100 Ways
to *Boost* Your
Self-Confidence

Believe in *Yourself*
and *Others* Will Too

BARTON GOLDSMITH, PhD
Author of *Emotional Fitness at Work*

CAREER
PRESS

Franklin Lakes, N.J.

100 WAYS TO BOOST YOUR SELF-CONFIDENCE
EDITED AND TYPESET BY KARA KUMPEL
Cover design by Lucia Rossman/DigiDog Design
Printed in the U.S.A. by Courier

To order this title, please call toll-free 1-800-CAREER-1 (NJ and Canada: 201-848-0310) to order using VISA or MasterCard, or for further information on books from Career Press.

CAREER
PRESS

The Career Press, Inc., 3 Tice Road, PO Box 687,
Franklin Lakes, NJ 07417
www.careerpress.com

Library of Congress Cataloging-in-Publication Data
Goldsmith, Barton.
        100 Ways to boost your self-confidence : believe in yourself and others will too /
by Barton Goldsmith.
        p. cm.
        Includes bibliographical references and index.
        ISBN 978-1-60163-112-1 -- ISBN 978-1-60163-745-1 (ebook) 1. Self-confidence. I.
Title. II. Title: One hundred ways to boost your self-confidence.

    BF575.S39G65 2010
    158.1--dc22

                                                            2010008878

To my clients, readers, and listeners.

To the thousands of people who have e-mailed,
written, and telephoned to share their personal
stories with me: I know for a fact that I
would not have had the confidence to write
this book, if it wasn't for your support.

Therefore I humbly dedicate it to
each and every one of you.

Acknowledgments

At Career Press, I'd like to thank Acquisitions Editor Michael Pye for asking me to write this book, and Production Coordinator James Plasky for his assistance and talent. I'd also like to thank Laurie Kelly-Pye for her outstanding PR and willingness to go the extra mile.

A great big thank-you to my literary agent, Katie Boyle, and assistant, Lauren Chen, for their efforts and support.

This book wouldn't exist if not for the readers of my column, and I will be forever grateful to the editors of the hundreds of publications that have graciously run my articles and allowed me to rant and elucidate. My editors at *The Ventura County Star*, where my column began, have truly launched my career and been nothing but kind. Many thanks to Assistant Managing Editor Mike Blackwell, Editor Julie Price, Editor & VP Joe Howry, Publisher George H. Cogswell, III, and the *VC Star* staff. In addition, I wish to acknowledge Bob Jones and his team at Scripps-Howard News Service for their unwavering support. I know I would not be where I am if not for their encouragement and faith.

The team (and my dear friends) at KCLU/NPR Radio have been incredibly supportive, innovative, and just plain fun to be around. They include General

Manager Mary Olson, Program Director Jim Rondeau, News Director Lance Orozco, Mia Karnatz-Shifflett, Stephanie Angelini, and Jocelyne Rohrback. A special thank you to my co-host, Dr. Stephen Trudeau, who is also my best friend, and kindly contributed both inspiration and a chapter for this book. In addition, I must acknowledge the many guests who have shared their wisdom with our listening audience. I feel as though I "get schooled," in the best sense, every week.

Thank you to my family and friends, including Keaton and Oliver Koechli, who are too wonderful for words, and my nephews, David and Daniel Richmond, who make me proud. Thank you to my assistant, Mary Trudeau, who makes my life work and reminds me to eat. Thank you also to Shelley MacEwen for reading anything I write and giving her unedited opinion, as well as my dear friends Michael Park and Kevin Connelly, Linda Gerrits, Jeb Adams, Leigh Leshner, Jim Cathcart, Diane and Dennis Merritt Jones, and Nancy and David Padberg.

I am honored to have learned from my colleagues in the (sometimes opposing) worlds of business, journalism, and psychology, including Gary Chapman, Marjory Abrams, Judith Orloff, Harville Hendrix, Bernie Siegel, Dan Maddux, Marci Schimoff, Susan Shapiro Barash, Kevin Hanley, Bambi Holzer, Karen Leland, Debra Mandel, Shel Horowitz, Ed Rigsbee, Pete Lakey, Brad Oberwager, Sietze and Nancy Vanderheide, John James, James Hollis, Helen Fisher, Joe Phelps, Larry Winget, Jeff Zeig, Shawn Christopher

Shea, Anne Sheffield, Gerald Jampolsky, William Glasser, Scott James, Linda Metzger, and Rick Welch.

Some of my mentors have passed on, but they all made the world a better place before they left: Albert Ellis, David Viscott, Elizabeth Kubler-Ross, and Indus Arthur.

I have had the privilege of being a resource for and working with a number of educational, leadership, and mastermind organizations (the best part is that I got to learn and grow right along with them): The Young Presidents Organization (YPO), The Young Entrepreneur's Organization (YEO), The World Presidents Organization (WPO), and Vistage (formally TEC, The Executive Committee).

I have also had the opportunity to speak to many businesses and associations around the world, and those experiences have helped to shape the ideas shared in this book. This list would be too long to print, but I thank you all, and I am honored that you continue to allow me to share my experiences, ideas, and a few jokes.

I also wish to thank those people and companies who have worked with me and given the greatest gift of all: their trust.

Thank you KJ, for a most unlikely, but wonderful friendship. And thanks to my friends at Firenze Osterio: Chef Fabio, Lisa, Tamara, Little Lisa, and John.

Lastly I must give some extra treats to Mercy the Wonder-Dog and Piewackett the Magical Cat for the gift of allowing me to rescue them and then rescuing me right back.

Contents

Introduction

Confidence Always Lies Somewhere Within

A person grows whenever he or she thinks, contemplates, and dreams. Your ideas, reflections, and even random thoughts can build your self-confidence, but you have to be aware of them to get the full benefit.

Research tells us that the human brain can think of five to nine things at the same time, so it can be a bit challenging to isolate and identify the confidence-building thoughts from those that do you no good.

Realizing that you have confidence within you, even if it has been hiding for a while, is the first step in reinforcing it. Deciding that you want to retain and focus on your self-confidence is the next one. By first finding it, you then have the ability to harness it.

For many who live with doubt, or are in challenging situations, believing that they are even capable of feeling confident can be difficult. I recommend that, if you are feeling this way, you find some quiet reflection time to help you see that somewhere inside you lies a confident thought or two. And that is all you need to get to the next level.

To get to this point, it can help to remember a time when you felt good about yourself and your life. Those are confident memories, and we all know that if you've done it before, you can do it again. Reflecting on past successes and allowing yourself to feel the positive emotions connected with them will help you create a greater ability to tap in to your confidence, because you aren't just wishing and hoping; you are seeing that you really have been (and can be) a more self-confident person.

Those little pieces of success, pride, and assurance are like seeds: If you plant them, give them a little sunlight and water (or in this case some time and thought), you will begin to feel better about yourself and what you are doing.

Even though this exercise doesn't involve lifting weights or even putting on your sneakers, it is a workout for your emotions. Initially most people are a little reluctant, partially because it's unfamiliar territory, which always produces a touch of anxiety. Pushing through your discomfort and actually working on identifying where your confidence lies is a task that, when completed, you will be thankful you took on.

Once you get in touch with the reality that you have the ability to believe in yourself (because you have had it before), your life will get a little easier and most likely a lot more fun.

Confidence isn't about taking over the world; it is about enjoying your world as much as possible. It doesn't take much, and you do have it inside your heart and soul, so take a little time and look for it. I think you will be more than pleased with yourself by what you find.

1. 10 Instant Confidence-Builders

*It's not that I'm so smart, it's just that
I stay with problems longer.*
—Albert Einstein

When things get out of control and you momentarily lose your confidence, there are any number of little things you can do to regain it. Here are 10 tools to help get you started.

1. Wash your hands and face, and brush your teeth. It cools your body, which is relaxing, and gives you that "fresh start" feeling.

2. Look at any diploma or certificate of achievement you have. And if it isn't framed and on the wall, do it now. These are reminders of your accomplishments, and taking in your success is important to maintaining your confidence.

3. Remember your last (or greatest) success and think about it for 60 seconds. Taking in your success as often as possible will help you reach another and another. Quite simply, it reminds you that, because you have done it before, you can do it again.

4. Give yourself a good shave (face or legs). It's another instant refresher, and, in addition, when we know we are looking our best, we are naturally more confident.

5. Know you are the person your kids or other loved ones think you are. Knowing that you are unconditionally loved can't help but make you feel good about yourself.

6. Wash your car, inside and out. Hey, when our wheels are shiny, we feel better. If you don't think this applies to you, just remember how you felt the last time you got a ride in someone's very funky car. Race you to the car wash.

7. Put on clean socks and shoes you haven't worn in a few days. Shoes take a day or two to release any moisture they have absorbed, and this is a very easy way to put a little pep back into your step.

8. Organize your closet and get rid of anything that no longer fits. Old clothes may come back into style, but you really don't want them on hangers for the next 20 years. Throwing out the old makes room for the new. For some, the feeling they get from putting on a new "power suit" fills them with self-esteem.

9. Cook a lovely meal. Even if you are by yourself, preparing a tasty dinner, setting the table, and treating yourself to a wonderful culinary experience will lift your spirits. Sharing it with someone you love and/or respect will make it even more nurturing.

10. Look around you, remember that you started with nothing, and know that everything you see, you created. We can all lose our feelings of self-worth, especially when something goes wrong

in our world. The real truth is that, if you have done it before, you can do it again. No matter what.

None of these tasks has to be uncomfortable, and won't take you much time. Finding ways to give yourself a little boost when you're not feeling at the top of your game is a trick that truly confident people use on a regular basis.

2. Negativity Kills Confidence

I was always looking outside myself for strength and confidence but it comes from within. It is there all the time.
—Anna Freud

Negative environments where people are harsh or even abusive to one another are toxic. No one tries to lift you or anyone else out of the pain, and no one can find emotional or even physical comfort—that will lower your self-worth and perhaps even your will to live.

This isn't about having the occasional bad day or moment. It's about living and/or working in an environment that brings or puts you down. When someone is constantly telling you that you're not good enough, eventually, if you stay around a while, you will start to believe it.

Only two creatures on the planet, if you continually tell them they are bad, will take it in and believe it: dogs and humans. We have all seen dogs whose spirits have been broken. They walk around with their tails between their legs and their heads down. They get startled or scared very easily, and can react with fear aggression (barking or growling when they are frightened). The poor things never seem to feel safe and secure. They have lost their wag, and it's sad to see.

People tend to react in similar ways when they are living with someone who puts them down on a regular basis or they are working for a company that manages by intimidation. There is very little joy to be found here, and one's sense of self-confidence can be easily shattered. Most people in such places are unable to find the strength they need to battle the forces that are attacking them because they have simply run out of energy.

The trick here is to step back far enough to get some perspective, and, if the circumstances I just described truly exist, and counseling hasn't worked or is refused, the best move may be to just leave. I know that's drastic, but staying in a negative environment or relationship because you are afraid to leave is also known as "battered person's syndrome," such as when abused women continue to go back to the home of their abusers. They do it because the devil they know is better than the one they don't (as they mistakenly think). They are returning to what is familiar.

Confidence cannot exist within an aura of meanness. To find yourself and rebuild what has been taken from you, leaving a bad environment may be the answer. This requires a type of inner strength that some find in desperate moments—the strength that helps you believe in yourself and to know that you do not deserve to be treated badly, no matter what another person says. You have finally had enough, and you reach down to the depths of your soul and pull up whatever shreds of self-respect you can find. The feeling may only last for a few hours, but use that time to pack or write your resignation, because you will never be able to flourish where negativity and horrific behavior are allowed to run rampant.

Once most people get out of a negative environment or relationship, one of the first things they do is castigate themselves by saying, "Why did it take me so long?" But that thought is totally self-defeating. It took as long as it took; do not waste any more time feeling beat up. At this point you may actually be used to it and not even see that you are doing it to yourself. As soon as you are aware you've changed the behavior, all you have to do next is whatever is in front of you. Leave the past, and the old behaviors, behind. Accept that you had the strength to change your life. It's okay to feel good about yourself.

3. Push Through the Upset

When you are going through hell—keep going.
—Winston Churchill

You had a great plan for the day ahead. You even went to bed early so you could wake up with a little more energy to put to your project du jour, but something happened. Somewhere in the night, upset struck your unconscious, or perhaps you got an early-morning phone call or nudge, and a problem you had not anticipated occurred. So much for your best-laid plans.

When the unexpected happens, we usually get a little anxious; sometimes we totally freak out. Again, this is pretty human stuff, but the problem is that whenever most people get derailed, their confidence is shaken, and they can change direction (or just get lost) and have difficulty getting back on track.

Here's an alternate way to keep your focus and move forward in the process: Instead of putting your project aside to deal with the problem that's trying to get your attention, take the time to do what you were going to do in the first place. By not allowing yourself to be thrown off course, you are keeping control. If you can sit down and complete your goal, despite your current (and most likely momentary) circumstances, you will build your self-confidence and won't lose any ground.

Being able to focus, even though you are stressed, and get the job done gives you the knowledge that, no matter what happens, you can avoid internal musings and excuses. Doing what needs to be done, regardless of temporary setbacks, will make you proud of yourself. It also produces a secondary positive outcome, which is a greater ability to focus on the problem that caused the upset, because you won't be thinking of what you haven't gotten done.

You will also gain more clarity, and maybe even some additional ideas of how to deal with your dilemma while finishing the work you had planned to do. Any time you can use your unconscious to help you create some problem-solving skills, do it. We have all experienced getting better ideas once our minds are actually off a problem we are trying to solve.

In addition, you may be able to channel your nervous energy into something much better. Just being frenetic and ignoring what you had planned to do doesn't help you or anyone else. But if those around you see that, even though the world is going to hell in a handbasket, you can still get the job done, then everyone involved feels more confident about you.

Sometimes putting out fires can be a way of avoiding what you really need to be doing. So make sure the emergency is real and you truly are needed before you put your priorities on the shelf. The truth is that you do have the ability to get your homework done *and* save the world.

4. A Secret to Happiness

Without a humble but reasonable confidence in your own powers you cannot be successful or happy.
—Norman Vincent Peale

I asked Marci Shimoff, author of the *New York Times* best-seller *Happy for No Reason* and featured teacher in *The Secret*, what she believed about how confidence and happiness are related, and how, together, they can help us create a life worth living fully.

Marci says:

I define true happiness as an inner state of peace and well-being regardless of circumstances. That's why I call it "happy for no reason." When we experience that kind of inner happiness, we also have high self-esteem—we believe in ourselves and know that we are worthy regardless of our circumstances. That is true confidence.

Developing the inner state of well-being will create confidence in all areas of your life. If you don't develop inner well-being, you may feel confident in one specific area of your life (perhaps you're confident in your intelligence), but uncomfortable in many other areas. That is "conditional confidence," and it will never bring you fulfillment.

Marci sees the process of developing greater confidence like building a muscle—it takes regular training, making a habit of doing the things that help you feel inner peace and well-being.

Marci also believes that it's important to listen to and learn from your inner guidance. She says, "Trust your intuition, as your inner wisdom will guide you to your greatest success and happiness in life. Believe in your wisdom and follow it."

For many of us, trusting ourselves may be difficult because we have been habituated to look outside of ourselves for our answers. So it's best to start out with small decisions for which you are listening to your own guidance. Then every success that comes from your own guidance reinforces your belief in yourself.

Marci goes on to say, "Any day of the week I will put my faith in someone who has unconditional confidence. They are open and willing to learn whatever they need because they have a fundamental belief in themself [sic]."

Marci's work has inspired millions of people to look within and not only find happiness, but along with it a stronger sense of self and a greater enjoyment of life. And with that, you can live happily and confidently every after.

5. Be Patient With Yourself

If you have confidence you have patience.
Confidence, that is everything.
—Ilie Nastase

If you don't reach your goals the first time you try, don't see it as a failure. Remember that you have learned something and will do better next time. The way to develop self-confidence is to know that, no matter what happens, you will grow from the experience.

It is easy to become impatient and frustrated, but just imagine what life would be like if Thomas Edison gave up trying to invent the electric light after failing thousands of times. He had lots of ideas and the patience to carry them out. When asked about the attempts that didn't work, Edison allegedly said something like, "I didn't fail 10,000 times; I just found 10,000 ways that *didn't* work."

Yes, as well as being patient, he was persistent, and the two do go together: One could say that you need to have the patience to be persistent, or vice versa. The real truth is that patience comes from a place of believing that you have the answers or trusting your ability enough that you know you will find them. That is the essence of self-confidence.

Self-confidence doesn't come from sitting on your hands and waiting for something to happen. It is about throwing everything you have against the wall and waiting (patiently) for something to stick. Then you have to take your time to refine your projects. For many, that is the hardest part of the process. Great innovators can be very impatient when it comes to the implementation of their ideas.

Remember that when you are being impatient with yourself, there is no one who can defend you. Our self-imposed "deadlines" really need to be changed to "preferred time lines." If you miss a deadline, it unconsciously creates anxiety because a part of your brain actually feels as though you will die if the job doesn't get done. That also happens when a person doesn't give you what you think you want, when you think you need it. Your mind is really telling you that you may lose something very important to you and that can cause some panic. When you are stressed in that way, getting anything done is more problematic.

Practicing patience, by forcing yourself to take your time, can also be done by realizing how you react with people you are close to. If you are impatient with them it is likely that you will be the same way with yourself, and that shows a lack of self-confidence. Learn how to be more patient with yourself when life gets in the way or requires more time than you budgeted, by working harder on going with the flow. If you feel yourself starting to get antsy, take a patience pill by simply reminding yourself that Rome wasn't built in a day, and whatever you are involved in is worth the time you are investing.

Patience may be a virtue, but it is also a necessity in achieving and living a self-confident life.

6. Be Prepared

The most difficult thing is the decision to act; the rest is merely tenacity. The fears are paper tigers. You can do anything you decide to do. You can act to change and control your life, and the procedure, the process is its own reward.
—Amelia Earhart

You can't feel confident unless you know what you need to know. Get educated, learn, research, and never stop reading. Preparing, whether it is for a presentation or a date, will help you feel safe and allow you to show off your best assets.

By making sure all your ducks are in a row you can also plan for the unexpected more easily. Although you may not have brought every trick in the book with you, you probably read about them at some point. If you prepare, it makes the inevitable question you were afraid of easy to answer.

No, you can't constantly be ready for everything life throws at you. But, getting into the habit of preparing, you create a backlog of emotional building blocks you'll get to use later. Trust me on this one, please; there is no wasted effort here. Whatever you are preparing for today, even if you don't use it tomorrow, you will in the future.

Preparing emotionally is as important as preparing mentally and physically. The best way I have found is to visualize (imagine in your mind's eye) what it is you are about to do. If it's taking a test, see yourself passing it. If it's giving a speech, see the audience nodding their heads and applauding (perhaps even laughing at your jokes). This technique is used to cure cancer, and I'm sure it can make you feel more self-confident. It will also help you succeed at the task in front of you.

Mental preparation requires that you are studied or have the ability to learn. There's an old joke about men never bothering to read instructions; that may have been the case before the technology revolution, but not these days. Life is way too complicated to not at least look at the manual before you try to hook up that new video-game system.

Doing common-sense preparation, such as a mental or written checklist before you begin a project, old or new, is only going to make you feel more confident about what you are about to take on. In addition, it will help you think of things you may have missed—and you won't be wondering what the leftover parts are for.

Making a checklist might seem a little over the top if you are just going out for dinner and a movie, but it can be immensely helpful when you are doing something as simple as going to the market. I don't know how anyone can get through life without to-do lists. They may actually be our single greatest aid when it comes to getting things done and staying on track.

If required, taking safety precautions is another great preparation technique: Carefully organizing your gear as you prepare to climb the Matterhorn in the Alps, you mentally practice using it. As you tee up your ball, and look around to make sure you're not going to pulverize your boss with your Big Bertha driver, you are also preparing yourself to make a great shot by reducing your anxiety.

Preparation is your friend, and not nearly as painful as you think it is. It is also a necessity when it comes to gaining greater self-confidence.

7. Recognition Is More Powerful Than Money

Wherever a man turns he can find someone who needs him.
—Albert Schweitzer

Having a sphere of influence and providing a place where others can build their own confidence also gives you a better life. It is how we generate the future and make our own lives full.

Everyone has baggage that keeps them from being the best they can be. Your job is to check those bags for them (or at least make sure they are carry-on). It will help to bring out the best of that person because he will understand that he is not doing it all alone. He will feel much better about himself and your conversation, as well as your connection with him.

Helping someone feel good about him or herself can be as simple as saying "Thanks." You would be surprised at how many people feel they go through their lives without recognition. A pat on the back, a handwritten thank-you note, and a small token of appreciation are just a few of the ways you can lift someone to a higher level without investing a ton of time and energy.

When was the last time you thanked your loved ones for just being part of your life? Have you recognized the people who work with you and help you make that part of your life as easy as possible? Then there are those whom we only see once in a while, or, in the digital age, *never* see. How do you let them know you appreciate their participation in your world? I make sure to write personal notes when it's appropriate and fully acknowledge their contribution to what I do.

I find that most people are pleased with the recognition, and I also feel good about myself for I thinking about doing it and following through. It can only help to make your relationships—personal or business—better. Giving confidence through recognition comes back to you in many ways.

Helping people feel better about themselves will foster good in every way, shape, and form. Give it a try. Your life, and the lives of those you recognize, will be better for it.

8. Embrace Your Fears

Courage is resistance to fear, mastery of fear, not absence of fear. Except a creature be part coward, it is not a compliment to say it is brave.
—Mark Twain

Logic would dictate that overcoming something that frightens you makes you stronger and more self-reliant. By embracing your fears, you are creating a much more efficient and practical way of dealing with them. You don't have to climb Mount Everest or jump out of a perfectly good airplane to move through your anxieties; oftentimes just dealing appropriately with the stress and worry of daily life can increase your self-confidence.

One of my friends is a successful physician who says that he is scared every day, and he welcomes it because he truly believes it makes him a better doctor. He is more careful and doesn't take unnecessary chances with his patients. It drives him to be his very best and makes him a more confident practitioner.

I was once told that faith is the opposite of fear, and whereas I see how having a belief in a higher power can make you feel safer, I also think that understanding why your fears exist, and learning the lessons they can teach us, are also very powerful tools.

For most of us there is a payoff to our fears. Yes, they can keep us physically safe so we don't step off a cliff or try to pet a tiger, but there is often more to our fears than just keeping ourselves protected. Fears can make us more introspective and help us see exactly where we need to make adjustments so that we have the strength to accomplish the task at hand. Having the confidence to wrap your head around your fears and look at how they help or hurt you is a great exercise to help you not only overcome them, but also use them to accomplish your goals.

If you want to be a leader, public figure, or movie star, but you have panic attacks at the very thought of speaking to a room full of people, attaining that goal will be quite difficult. However, you can realize your (apparent) weakness and do something about it, for instance, joining Toastmasters (*www.toastmasters.org*). Not only will you get the tools you need to succeed, but you will also build a skill that will help you reach your vision, and make you more confident in the process.

Admitting to yourself that you have a fear of speaking in public (which is the number-one fear in humanity) allows you to drop any pretense you may have had and feel good about getting better at it.

I don't know anyone who has overcome or embraced their fears and not been better off and more confident for it. Whatever it is that scares the hell out of you should be tackled with the insight that, by hitting it head-on, you will vanquish the demons that reside in your mind.

9. Find a Mentor

Confidence is a very fragile thing.
—Joe Montana

If you didn't have the kind of parenting that helped you develop self-confidence, it's not too late. Find someone you respect, in a field you can love, and ask that person to be your mentor. Most people are flattered by the request and will do what they can to help you.

Mentoring isn't therapy or even life coaching. It is a process by which someone who has more knowledge and experience in certain areas than you, and who is willing to share what she has learned, helps you navigate the rapids of work and life.

The first step, after you've found each other, is to discuss and agree on the nature and goals of your relationship. This conversation will set the tone for your future endeavors together, so take your time with it.

You can have mentors for a number of areas in your life. A mentor on the job can be worth his or her weight in gold. Your relationship mentor can help guide you through the inevitable ups and downs of life with another person. You can even have a fishing or tennis mentor, which is different from taking lessons because the mentor is there for your overall well-being, not just to teach you how to "be better at it."

For example, I do not play competitive tennis; I play/mentor what I have come to call *Zen tennis*. The object of this game is to hit the ball in such a way that your partner (not opponent) can easily return it and keep the volley going as long as possible. The point is to play, not merely to win. It's a great way of getting exercise and refining your aim and intention on the court. Besides, it's fun, it's good practice, and no one walks away feeling as though they've lost. It's a great confidence builder.

Having a mentor in any area of your life can be valuable. I seldom see mentor/mentee relationships that don't work out for the best. Everyone eventually outgrows their mentor, and then the relationship morphs into something else, but the bond that was created will not go away (unless you want it to). The good news here is that you can always pick up the phone and give your mentor a ring if you're dealing with something you'd like to run by him.

The confidence you get from having someone nearby whom you trust, who knows what she is doing, and knows who you are, is a tremendous gift. If you have never had a mentor, it's not too late. If it's been a while, then maybe getting another one is a good idea, because the problems we face in the world today are not going away; they are just getting more complicated.

When confusion strikes, and we don't know what to do in the moment, it rattles our self-confidence. Talking with a mentor is a great way to reinforce your abilities and remind you that you have the smarts and the skills, as well as another person to help you vanquish the challenges of life and love.

More information on mentoring is available in my book *Emotional Fitness at Work*, also published by Career Press.

10. Maintain the Machine

Self-respect permeates every aspect of your life.
—Joe Clark

Staying healthy by exercising, getting enough rest, and watching your diet keeps your energy level high.

It's hard to feel good about yourself when you're running on empty.

For some people, self-care is the last thing on their to-do list, which doesn't help you cut it in the real world. If you don't maintain the machine (you), it becomes more difficult to attract and attain your dreams and desires. The things you want will become elusive, and you won't like yourself or your life very much.

By taking care of yourself, you make it easier for positive experiences to be a part of your life, because, quite simply, like attracts like, and feeling good brings good things to you. It sounds easy—and it is—but it requires that you like who you are and feel that you deserve some of the goodies the world still has to offer.

By becoming an Olympic-level couch potato, you can't put out the energy required to make things happen. The truth is that, when you are tired, getting anything done or keeping things in proper order becomes arduous. We've all had days when we just didn't want to get out of bed. Imagine where you would be if you did that nearly every day. It's pretty hard to make anything happen when you can't get up until the crack of noon.

Energy can be enhanced with proper self-care. If you don't know what to do, just start with the basics: Take a walk, cut out the Haagen-Dazs, and go to sleep at a decent hour. Much more information about self-care is available online, and there are countless books on the subject, but most of it is common sense.

If you're really struggling with self-care, you may have a little depression going on, and you should get it checked out before embarking on a fitness plan. Your emotional well-being has to be fully functioning for you to be able to take better care of your physical body.

The fear of doing something new or different can keep you locked in its grip if you don't fight your way out. Sometimes it helps to make strong demands of yourself, but you can't force the issue. This is where getting a personal trainer or joining a gym can be helpful. Upon occasion, we all need someone to inspire us (or kick us in the butt) to get our bodies moving and our hearts pumping, and to start making healthy choices.

Sometimes we just get into a bad pattern. Not taking care of ourselves first becomes a habit, then a lifestyle. If you think you are there, it's really time to make some changes.

So put down that cigar or candy bar, pick up a bottle of water, change into your walking shoes, and hit the pavement. Not only will you feel better about yourself, but you may just make a few new friends who are also committed to getting healthy.

11. Clarity Creates Confidence

Clarity affords focus.
—Thomas Leonard

Knowing that you know, that feeling of being absolutely, positively *right*, deep inside yourself, is truly empowering. To get to that place you have to clear away any issues that could block your progress by checking in with your mind and emotions, and learning to trust your feelings.

If you are facing a problem, the first thing you need to do is to ask yourself "clarifying questions." The easiest way to know what questions you need to ask is to imagine that someone is trying to help you out, and he or she will need some clarification on what the issue is. Now ask yourself those same questions. It can help to write down both the questions and your answers.

Look at the problem from every angle possible; sometimes it helps to actually run it by a person you trust and see what he thinks. He may come up with other questions and help you create more clarity. Then, once you can see what the real issues are, you can begin to create solutions.

Clarifying questions can be anything from *how much?* to *how long?*, and even *why are we doing this?* Don't limit yourself—this exercise doesn't cost you a thing and will give you the information you need to make an informed decision, and be confident in it.

Learning to ask the right questions of yourself will save you money and time as well as give you a feeling of empowerment.

12. Be Open to New Ideas

Confidence, like art, never comes from having all the answers; it comes from being open to all the questions.
—Earl Gray Stevens

Being open to new ideas when you are looking to solve a problem is what true learning (as well as confidence-building) is all about. Believe in your own resources and those of people you trust.

If you try to do it all yourself, micro-manage every detail, and don't welcome new and innovative ideas from those around you, it's gonna be hard to make it to the next level, or even survive where you currently are.

It is always wise to get some input from the competent people with whom you've surrounded yourself. Unless you want to live in a cabin in the middle of nowhere, without a connection to the modern world, you are going to be influenced by everything and everyone around you. Accept the influence, allow it to become a part of you, and let it make you the best you can be. Just be sure to give credit to those people who inspired you.

It makes sense: If you're secure with yourself, telling someone she had a great idea that you'd like to incorporate would be taken as a compliment. And the truth is that their idea actually did complement yours.

Sometimes the "off the wall" thought, the one you were just messing around with, is the one that makes the biggest impact. I call it playing with ideas; when you do it with other people, you might call it brainstorming. Sometimes someone says something just to be funny or to get a reaction (kids are great at that) and it turns out to be a concept that you totally resonate with.

Sometimes the answers or ideas you need do come from your own head, and you may ignore them if you are being hard on yourself, or your confidence tank is running dry. Learning to be open to your own thoughts, especially during difficult times, is a challenge we all face.

If you are not open to different types of intelligence (ideas from the world around you, and learning by living), your experience and your self-confidence will be greatly limited.

13. Nobility

To whom much is given, much is asked.
—Anonymous

Knowing that you are a person of honor and integrity keeps you on a purposeful and positive path. Those who have strong moral fiber are generally very confident people. This is because the foundation of their values is unshakable.

There is a big difference between knowing the right thing to do and just doing what you *say* is right. Wars have been fought over righteousness, but this isn't about forcing your beliefs on others. Nobility is a character trait that compels us to do the best thing for all concerned. When we think in that way, we can never lose.

If you feel that what is good for those around you is also good for you, then you've created a balanced and confident life. When a noble person sees a friend, loved one, or business associate succeed, it brings up a feelings of joy; envy is never part of the equation. People who possess the quality of nobility know that the good that comes to others will also affect them in a positive way. They also believe in helping people because it always comes back and makes your circle (of people and influence) stronger.

The "nobles" of days gone by, the good lords and ladies, worked to make the lives of those in the kingdom better. They realized that not everyone could care for themselves, and a little guidance and assistance was a good thing to give. Knowing the outcome of putting out positive energy makes it easier to do, and also gives you the sense that your purpose in life is greater than you may have suspected.

People who have noble aspirations enjoy doing the right thing and don't expect much in return. They have chosen to use to the gifts they were handed in a good way, and "pay it forward."

When you employ a noble attitude and your focus is toward the "highest good," your sense of self and confidence will get stronger, and you will get more out of life. A wonderful, unmistakable feeling comes from doing the right thing, and that feeling can only come from taking action to help your fellow humans.

Learning that you can't play the game of life solely for yourself is not a maturity thing, and it's how we can all contribute to make the world a better place. Once that happens, your life also gets better. Nobility is a win-win.

14. Strong Foundations

The will to do springs from the knowledge that we can do.
—James Allen

When you have a good foundation you have the knowledge, strength, and self-confidence necessary to create anything you want, and go wherever you like. This is a basic truth recognized by those who have accomplished their dreams.

Even if you don't have everything you need right now, there is nothing wrong with reviewing, relearning, or rehearsing to make your foundation as strong as possible. Self-confident people know (and are comfortable realizing) what they don't know, and take the steps necessary to get the information and support they need.

If you think of building your life the way you build a house, it can help you see how important having a strong foundation is. The very first thing you do when constructing a home is decide what kind of foundation you want and need. Similar decisions are required if you are starting a new business; you have to do your due diligence and make sure you have the right bankers, brokers, and business consultants, the foundation of any new venture. If the team and structure are in place, everything fits together so that your home, business, or new life has a good launching pad.

All people, homes, and businesses need regular maintenance, and perhaps even serious repairs along the way—these don't mean you have failed; these are things that happen over time. Most contractors will tell you that if your house has good bones (a strong foundation) you can make whatever repairs you need, or even remodel or expand. This goes for the rest of your life as well.

Judging yourself harshly because something didn't go right (welcome to the human race) won't help you out of your problem. Relying on the foundation of what you know you can accomplish makes dealing with any unforeseen problem much easier. If you have the right tools, such as confidence in what you are doing, or the availability of a dynamite support structure and team, you can move through whatever issue is presenting itself at the moment.

Having a good foundation doesn't require that you have a traditional education; you can rely on your talents, your experiences, and the abilities others to create the life, job, or home that you desire. Our foundations can come from anywhere. Perhaps your dad taught you how to construct and fix, or maybe your mom gave you a talent and desire to decorate, and you've always been good at it, but never really knew quite why. The reason is that you have a strong foundation, whether inherited, natural, or learned, and respecting it is a foundation for greater self-confidence.

15. Multiple Intelligences

Trust yourself. Then you will know how to live.
—Johann Wolfgang Von Goethe

Having the mental capital to invest in your ideas, the hard work ahead, or your interpersonal relationships gives you a leg up on those who do not. If you don't have the confidence that you possess the smarts you need to make your life work, there are other intelligences you can access that are just as (if not more) useful than your brainpower, and none of them require a college degree.

First, it may be necessary to reevaluate how you feel about intelligence. The reality of multiple intelligences has become widely accepted; it's not just about IQ anymore. Employers, evaluators, and educators now look at EQ (emotional intelligence) and CQ (creative intelligence) as well as a few others when evaluating talents and abilities.

I was not the top student in my class; that distinction belonged to my buddy Dr. Sitze Vanderheide, JD (yes, a doctor and a lawyer), and his lovely wife, Nancy, also has two Psy.D. degrees (doctorates in clinical psychology) and is president of the Los Angeles Psychoanalytic Institute of Contemporary Psychoanalysis (talk about your overachievers). Although they both would kick my butt in an intelligence test, we agreed that I'd score higher in creativity—and who would argue with the likes of them?

I share this anecdote to help you understand the importance of being able to see your whole self and not just one component. Very few of us can be doctors and/ or lawyers, let alone both. Just because you're not the smartest student in the class doesn't mean you can't be the most creative person in the workplace.

Continuing to compare yourself to someone who may have scored better on a test or gotten a higher degree makes life more difficult. Does he know how to navigate his life as well as you do? Does she accept who she is and feel confident about herself? These questions won't be found on the SATs, but your answers really show how you score in this game called Life.

You have all the intelligences you need, and your talents and abilities in other areas more than make up for what you think you might lack. Think about it, and also know that if you don't start believing in yourself, the gifts you have may become a little stale. Don't let a false belief keep you from forging ahead to make your world and the one we all share a better place.

16. Depend on Yourself

*There are only two things in life you
can count on: death and taxes.*
—Mark Twain

When you know you can count on those you
love, those who are on your team, and perhaps most
importantly yourself, you have the tools you need to
get through a rough patch or create something new
and wonderful in your life.

Trying to do it alone in the world today isn't
impossible—it will just take you a very, very long
time. Having someone to depend on makes your life
easier, and you also get the confidence that comes from
knowing that you don't have to do it all by yourself.

If you are a dependable person, taking pride in that
fact only makes you more reliable and confident because
you like the energy you're experiencing. It trickles into
your brain and helps you feel good about yourself, the
task you are working on, and the people you are helping
or those who are assisting you. It all becomes a positive
force. When a group of people work well together on a
project there is an *esprit de corps* that develops, and you
all get to share in good vibes.

Being the dependable one isn't boring; in fact, in
time it will make you more desirable. As we mature,
we tire of being let down or of people who are flakes.
You can win the heart of your true love or climb the
ladder of success if people know they can depend on

you. And when you truly realize that you can depend on yourself, then there isn't a river you can't cross or a problem you can't think your way out of. Confidence comes from knowing that you, or the person you need, will be there—period.

17. Like Riding a Bike

Experience is the best teacher.
—Anonymous

Having been there (and gotten the T-shirt) lets you know that you can go there again and again. Even if it has been years, most things in life are like riding a bike: You may be a little unsteady when you first try again, but the ability returns quickly.

Experience may be the most powerful force in building self-confidence. Once you know you're good at something, though you may have a bad day or two, you know deep in the core of your being that you can get back to where you were, and continue to improve. This is something the stand-outs in athletics, medicine, the arts, and leadership all have in common.

They also share the drive to constantly get better, and spend hours practicing, researching, and getting themselves in shape to do and be their best. I'm sure the Manning brothers don't stop throwing a football just because the season is over. Sure, it's important to take a break, but if you love what you do, and you love being one of the best, you won't be able to avoid picking up that ball and seeing if you can hit your favorite receiver.

What many may call "practice" is actually experience. Think about it: You run plays over and over in your head, you practice avoiding getting sacked, and you get in shape to run your hardest. This is all experience, and it all makes you better at what you do and who you are.

For those just starting their careers or in the middle of them, doing more of what intimidates you will help you get over the fear. You don't get used to it, but you come to understand what you need to do and believe that you can accomplish the task in front of you. Not only does the job become less anxiety-producing, but you will actually be able to master the task sooner than you may have thought.

Being experienced is not the same as being a burnout. Those who have a ton of experience in their fields are the "go-to" people who know things others have forgotten or never learned. The older doctor has seen things in his practice that a new doc, who may be aware of the latest technology, may not have experienced. When it comes to the cure, yes, I want to know what the latest inventions are, but when it comes to diagnosis, I'd rather be with a professional who has seen it before.

Remember: The more you do it, the easier it will be to repeat it. If you have many successes, it's easier to have them again.

18. Is It Need or Want?

Necessity is the mother of invention.
—Anonymous

Where would we be without our mothers, especially the mother of invention? Finding a need and filling it is one of the best ways to make yourself indispensable. In addition, being needed is one of life's greatest motivators and confidence-builders. If you have the energy to give of yourself when needed, it can only serve to boost the confidence others have in you, and it will be next to impossible not to feel a little better about yourself in the process.

Knowing the difference between what you need and what you want is important knowledge to have in order to make appropriate decisions. One of the easiest ways to look at it is by understanding the difference between hunger and appetite. When you feel hunger, your body is running low on calories and energy, and it wants to be fed, so your stomach sends a message to your brain that says "Feed me!" Appetite, however, is the desire for food that smells or looks tasty. You aren't starving and may not even need to eat, but you crave the savory scents and salivate at the anticipated flavor.

Now that you have a basic understanding of the difference, let's see how it relates to how you look at your own necessities versus your desires.

Start by doing a "necessity triage," which will help you decide what is a need and then put your wants in an appropriate place. List the things you think you need, and really be honest with yourself. Are they really needs, or just wants? I believe you will find that much of what you thought you needed was really a want, and you already have 99 percent of what you need. That in itself is a great confidence-builder. In addition, knowing that your needs are taken care of will allow you to give of yourself because you know that you can emotionally, physically, and financially afford to do so.

Also remember that the father of invention is perspiration, so be prepared to work for your desires.

19. Real Courage

Confidence is courage at ease.
—Daniel Maher

Courage is not the absence of fear; it is about moving through the unsure moments to reach your goals, despite any anxieties. Facing challenges with the understanding that you have the emotional mettle to withstand the difficulties around the corner is a building block of confidence.

Awareness of your surroundings and the realization that your path is the right one will help you get through many issues, both personal and professional. Think about it like a road trip (or a commute if you live in Los Angeles): When you're driving on the freeway, how many cars ahead do you look? If it's only at the car right in front of you, chances are you won't see the accident that occurred half a mile ahead, and all the cars in front of you slamming on their breaks. If you looked that half-mile in front of you, you would have avoided rear-ending someone because you would have seen the accident in plenty of time.

Courageous people are in touch with what is going on around them. They sense when things change and are usually prepared internally and externally to deal with changes and challenges. The brave give the impression that they are used to dealing with scary situations, but the truth is most just trust that they're doing the right thing, and if, for some reason, they find themselves in an unknown predicament, they improvise, using what they have around them. Perhaps courageous people are more resourceful than brave, but whatever the key, their confidence does depend on having the ability to monitor their surroundings and stay calm enough to deal with what comes their way.

When you know you're doing the right thing, it makes you feel empowered. And that kind of confidence can't help but give you the courage you need to face adversity. Whether it's a physical illness, a work challenge, or a relationship issue, if you trust that you are meant to be where you are, or meant to survive whatever is threatening you, your ability to win is greatly enhanced.

Courage comes from many places; it is with confidence that you can survive something that intimidates you. Maybe it's a new sport, a first date, or a new class—all of these things create anxiety in most people. No one wants to look bad to their friends who are watching, to a potential beau, or to a room full of people eager to learn. We all feel the same way, and knowing that should give you strength when it comes to tackling something different or a little scary.

The truth is, you've come this far and learned a bunch of new things, you've survived a few tragedies, and your mettle has been tested in a number of ways. That should give you the confidence that you will not only survive the new, but also gain the courage to try some things that may be much further out of your box than you may have reached before.

20. Sheepskin Confidence

The height of your accomplishments will
equal the depth of your convictions.
—William F. Scolavino

Knowledge is power. If you get educated, and really learn what you are taught, no human being can throw you off track because your connection to what you know is solid—a surefire confidence-booster if ever there was one.

Don't get me wrong; there are many educated people who just sit on their brains and do nothing with their lives. It is not just about going through the motions, reading the books, and passing the tests.

Getting educated is a process that makes you a broader, better, and brighter individual, and it doesn't have to be a traditional education either.

Learning a craft or art form, starting a business, and going to school are all forms of education. They are all things that will add to the fabric of your humanity and help you weave an inspiring tapestry of life. Education makes you more of what you already are, and may also help you uncover some gifts you didn't even know you had.

I've enjoyed some mild artistic success and learned how to write in the process. My business pursuits have always been great teachers—perhaps humbling at times, but always growth-producing. And I loved going to graduate school a little later in life. Not starting until I was in my 30s gave me a leg up because my life experience allowed me to gain greater insight in areas that were important and not take so seriously the things that didn't really matter.

That being said, the experience of receiving my diploma really did have a visceral effect on me. Simply put, I felt great about myself and my accomplishments. The degree helped me believe in myself like nothing else ever had. I knew that if I could do this, I could do whatever else I wanted. I remember it clearly, and am using the energy I got from it to write this book, the ones that preceded it, and the others that will follow.

The confidence that I and many, many others have gained from our educations is obvious, but not to be taken for granted. It was work, it cost money, and it took the most valuable thing we all have: time. There is no question that it was worth it, and the only thing I would do differently is perhaps be a little less openly opinionated in class (that way I wouldn't piss off as many teachers). But it was in those classrooms that I learned that *cocky* and *confident* are two very different things.

No matter what stage of life you are in, getting educated is one of the greatest gifts you can give to yourself.

21. Doing the Impossible

What we need are more people who specialize in the impossible.
—Theodore Roethke

On July 16, 2009, 17-year-old Zac Sunderland completed his 13-month journey to become the youngest person ever to circumnavigate the globe. In addition, he did it in a 36-foot boat, *Intrepid*, for which he paid $6,000 that he earned himself doing whatever he could. Talk about your confidence-builders.

I listened to Zac speak about his epic adventure in our hometown at the Westlake Yacht Club, which sponsored his epic travels along with the American Sailing Association. The poise and confidence displayed by this young man were far beyond his years.

I'd guess that spending so much time alone, avoiding modern-day pirates (with the help of the Australian Coast Guard), weathering storms with 30-foot waves, and eating canned and freeze-dried food that he described as "nasty" couldn't help but make you feel that you could do anything.

He also shared that he only caught about three fish, encountered sharks while swimming in the middle of nowhere, and stopped at about 14 ports along the way. Zac's impression of people in other cultures was that they were much more laid back than we are here at home.

He kept a blog, and many followed his journey via the Web. When he arrived at Marina del Rey, in Southern California, this cool kid was greeted by about 1,500 fans, 100 boats, 75 news media personnel, three helicopters, and an interview on *Jimmy Kimmel Live!*, with much more to come.

Although a bit overwhelmed by the media frenzy, he handled it well. But would you expect less from someone who just did the impossible? Fewer than 250 people have ever sailed solo around the globe. What an amazing club to belong to, let alone to be the youngest member of such an esteemed group of spirited souls.

Of course, one has to ask what gave him the courage to do it, and Zac's parents are a big part of the answer. The support they showed in his quest from the very beginning helped to give him the strength and confidence to complete the arduous journey.

"Zac is a very good sailor, and brave. We knew he could do it," said his mother, Marianne. Both his parents seemed mostly glad just to have him back home safe, and everyone is wondering what he's going to do next.

"I still have three courses to take to finish high school, and right now I just want to hang out with my friends," said Zac. It's easy to see him kicking it with his crew at the beach, now forever famous, but still, like, totally, a 17-year-old dude.

One explanation of how and why he was able to deal with the isolation during the nearly 28,000-mile journey was that he is the oldest of six siblings, and maybe he enjoyed a little privacy.

About six weeks after his epic adventure, a British sailor, Mike Perham, who was about three months younger than Zac, completed a solo circumnavigation of his own. But Zac will always hold the record for being the first person under 18 to cross the finish line.

No one is sure what Zac will do next, but his heart is attached to adventure, and he has earned the confidence to tackle his next great quest, whatever it may be. What is your next voyage?

22. Isolation Is Hazardous

When you are alone you are all your own.
—Leonardo Da Vinci

The statistics proving that people who cohabitate with others live longer than those who live alone have been around for several decades. In addition, more recent research has discovered that living in isolation may be more destructive to your physical well-being than smoking cigarettes. This doesn't mean that if you are happily enjoying the single life you're going to die prematurely, but it should make you think about life and love a little differently.

We are not meant to be alone. Just the fact that there are a few billion people on the planet is testament to that. Still, millions of folks who have been hurt or traumatized by one of their fellow humans may prefer to avoid contact with other *Homo sapiens*.

Those who have survived conflict-heavy relationships may well find it easier to just take care of themselves and perhaps their children or pets. Dealing with another person's vicissitudes can be exhausting, especially if that individual also gives you a hard time in the process.

However, if you enjoy sharing your life and bed with someone but also require your space, you need to get creative and discover some of the many ways to maintain your individuality and sanity while having a close relationship with another adult.

Many couples not living together take "nights off"; they have established safe boundaries that allow them to have their own time without making their partner insecure. Usually a phone call before the night off, followed by a catch-up conversation ("Did you sleep well?"), is enough to maintain a good connection.

If the person you love withdraws on a regular basis, and you have to go hunting for him or her, I suggest you have a deep conversation about the behavior and see what the cause is. This kind of action can make you feel abandoned, and that will take away from the depth of your love.

If you isolate as a means of getting back at someone, you are also hurting yourself. This passive-aggressive behavior may feel right in the moment, but after a little time has passed, you will feel lonely because you never shared what it was that hurt you in the first place. And if you don't talk about what bothers you, it will never stop.

Those who sequester themselves may also be dealing with depression and/or anxiety; they believe an illusion that being alone makes it all better. Not everyone who chooses to be alone has a mood disorder, but if you're also a little blue, you should get yourself checked out by a professional.

Being disconnected from the rest of the human race may make you feel safe or empowered, but it's a temporary feeling. In addition, it is hard to feel confident when there's no one around to validate your existence. We are social beings, and life is much more meaningful when you have someone to share it with.

23. Living a Good Life

*When you engage in systematic, purposeful action, using
and stretching your abilities to the maximum, you cannot
help but feel positive and confident about yourself.*
—Brian Tracy

There is a scene at the end of *Saving Private Ryan* in which the aged, rescued soldier tearfully asks his wife if he has lived a good life. Knowing that we have left the world a little better than we found it is the essence of self-worth and real happiness. Not the kind you get from a trip to Disneyworld, but from knowing deep inside of yourself that you've made a difference.

Don't underestimate it. The power of contribution, of being part of something that adds to the fabric of your community or the world, is a very healing action for everyone involved. It results in improved emotional health and stronger relationships, and it helps to build your internal 401k. You may not make actual cash, but you are investing in your self-worth, and that generally pays better dividends.

Living a good life doesn't mean that you have to be Volunteer of the Year, and it doesn't mean you have to sacrifice things you love or need. It means that you listen to your inner voice when it tells you that you have the ability to help someone in need.

Most of us can't pack up our lives and go to Africa to assist with relief efforts, but I think we all have the ability to do a little something and give those less fortunate a hand (versus a handout). Right now, giving money may not be possible, but you can offer your ideas, emotional support, and perhaps your personal e-mail list. Finding ways to get others involved is also a good use of your efforts, and it may be just the excuse you need to reconnect with some old friends.

When a worthy cause touches my heart, I have a short list of people I call to ask for assistance (usually a donation), and that way I can make a slightly larger impact. It may seem counterintuitive, but these folks actually welcome the calls. They, like many of us, want to be part of the solution, simply because it feels good to know you have made a difference.

Our sense of self is enhanced when we give to others. It generates brain chemicals that actually reduce depression and anxiety, as well as increase our capacity for joy. I have seen many a curmudgeon smile at the fact that they have given a person they may never see again a reason to hope. When you are struggling or just feeling down, the smallest offering from a stranger can make a big difference in your life. If you've ever been there, you know.

Living a good life isn't about how much you give; it's about giving in a way that will mean something to you. It doesn't have to be money or material. Sometimes the most valuable things you can offer are a kind word and an outstretched hand.

24. People Improve

Every day, in every way, I am getting better and better.
—Emile Coue

People improve. I see it every day. And most of the time, they do it on their own. Therapy can help, but the old saying does prove true more times than not: To make it really happen, you have to want to change.

Seeing a therapist can be beneficial, especially if the therapist is a good listener. Simply knowing that someone hears you completely is very empowering, and that is a doorway to positive transition.

That being said, I believe that we have the ability to change many things about ourselves on our own—without ever going to a counselor's office or even picking up a self-help book.

The first step, which is the most difficult, is to realize that a change is necessary or desirable. This can be the most arduous part, because it's hard to look at your own flaws.

Sometimes all that is required is a mild life-affirming (or life-altering) experience. Carl Jung would have called it a "spiritual experience." Unfortunately, this idea has gotten kind of a bad rap. When most people hear "spiritual experience," they immediately conjure up some kind of huge occurrence, such as a near-death experience, or losing someone very dear to them.

The truth is that profound depth can be found in the simplest of things. And many times, just realizing that you want things to be different can be the turning point in any number of difficult circumstances.

One of the best ways to make improvements in your own life is to look at how someone you respect changed for the better. Examining how those we admire have improved their circumstances can teach us what it is we need to do to enhance our own lives. If you'd like some advice, ask for it. People who take their own lives and behaviors seriously are usually willing to lend a hand, but don't expect them to come to you.

By making the effort to ask for guidance, you are showing your commitment to self-improvement. If someone is going to offer her counsel, she will want to know you're sincere.

Another way to make appropriate changes is to process what's happening internally. Sitting quietly and feeling what is going on inside of yourself is a tried and true way of healing your hurt and discovering what you need, so you can move on to the next level. The simplest form of meditation is to focus on your breath (inhaling and exhaling) for several minutes. This also has been proven to promote happiness.

There are millions of ways to make yourself feel better, but they all require the same thing to work: You have to want them to, and you have to embrace the changes.

25. The Power of Positive Thinking

*People become really quite remarkable when they start
thinking that they can do things. When they believe
in themselves they have the first secret of success.*

—Norman Vincent Peale

From time to time, we all think and say negative
things to ourselves. It's relatively normal. Unfortunately,
when thinking this way becomes a regular habit, it can
keep you from enjoying life, reaching your goals, or
even finding love.

One of the ways to break this habit is to become aware
of the negative thoughts while they are happening. This
kind of mindfulness can turn the experience into a positive
one. Being conscious of what's going on inside your head
and around your life really helps reduce your tension.

If you know you're stressed out, try taking a
patience pill. Do that by telling yourself that you need
to go with the flow until the uncomfortable, negative
thoughts or moments pass.

Many times we think in the negative when we're
not feeling good about ourselves. Perhaps your boss,
partner, or parents got on your case or didn't come
through with a promise, leaving you feeling low. In real
life, this is sometimes hard to avoid.

But being aware of how you are really feeling in
the moment gives you the ability to change the energy
and protect yourself by purposely thinking positive
thoughts. This is not the same thing as being a
Pollyanna. Using your own brain to help you resolve a

difficult moment is a tried and true technique that will assist you in shifting your mood.

Appreciating where you are and what you have also helps. You also need to commit to yourself that you're not going to let painful emotions or situations run your life or suck you in. Use the power of positive thinking to keep a bad moment from becoming a lifestyle.

Here are some additional tips to help you get started:

- Make a mental list of what is working in your life. This helps set the tone for moving through a difficult time. Then look at how you've dealt with other challenges for additional internal support.

- Remember "The Little Engine That Could?" Say to yourself, "I think I can." Or, "I know I can" may work even better.

- When you catch yourself thinking, "I'm not good enough," stop the negative thought and actually say, "I'm canceling that out." Then make a positive statement, such as "I've succeeded before and I can do it again," in its place.

Another reason to put a plus-sign in your mind's minus column is that negative thoughts take energy away from you while positive ones give you more. Just do the math and you can see it's worth the effort.

Negative thinking isn't just a bad habit; it can do real harm to you and your loved ones, especially if you (or they) start to believe it. So turn off that downer station in your head and tune in to the good things you do and have. Your world will be better for it.

26. Procrastination

*Put all excuses aside and remember
this: YOU are capable.*
—Zig Ziglar

*I've been meaning to get around to this for a while,
but it's so easy to find other things to do.* That is the credo
of the procrastinator. Don't get me wrong; I believe
that if it weren't for the last minute, nothing would get
accomplished. But if you are making yourself miserable
because you can't bring yourself to do what you need
to do, it's time to change that habit. Here are some tips
to help you do just that.

Timing is everything. Start timing how long it
takes you to do some of the things you procrastinate
about. For example, the man in my mirror hates doing
dishes. I used to let them pile up in the sink. Then one
day, I was in a hurry and happened to glance at the
clock before I began putting my hands in soapy water.
When I was finished, I looked at the clock again, and
all of six minutes had passed. Now that I know the
process takes much less time than all the things I did
to avoid it, getting it done is much easier. And life at
home is a bit more pleasant.

Just do it. Some Olympic-level procrastinators will
spend much of their time trying to look for shortcuts or
employing avoidance techniques such as saying "That's
not my job," or thinking "Who else can I get to do
this?" The truth is that if you just jump into the task at

hand, you will have some extra time in your life, which you can use in whatever way you choose.

Face your fear. When you've been avoiding something because the thought of the task or failing at it causes you anxiety, it can't feel good. In addition to fighting the fear factor, you are actually creating an excuse to delay or completely disregard important things in your life. If you are scared of a particular chore, it will help to get your partner or a friend to assist you. For many people, just having the company is a great motivator. Fear can block us from many things in life; working through it will strengthen you and your relationships.

Schedule lazy time. Often we don't get around to doing what we need to do because we're just plain tired. One of the best ways to overcome this is to reward yourself with a nap or some downtime once you have completed what you need to do. Taking a break is a necessity; none of us can be productive all the time, and getting a good rest actually makes you sharper.

Getting past procrastination is a good thing, but you need not beat yourself up in the process. You didn't create this behavior overnight, and it won't go away just because you've thought about it. Take steps, one at a time, to move your life forward, and before you know it, you will love the productivity and your life a lot more.

27. Respond Instead of React

Fight for your opinions, but do not believe that they contain the whole truth, or the only truth.
—Charles A. Dana

Responding rather than reacting will prevent you from experiencing or causing a lot of unnecessary pain.

What happened the last time you just reacted without thinking? Did you yell at someone who is important to you? Did it take several hours or days to recover and let things get back to normal? Did you think, in retrospect, that you could have chosen to respond differently?

Most people who go into reaction mode are driven by fear, and with the recent economic meltdown, a lot of folks in all walks of life are feeling anxious to one degree or another. That anxiety is a hair trigger for a reaction that may damage a relationship. Looking at how you react to a difficult or threatening situation is the first step in changing this difficult dynamic.

When you react, you are becoming a victim and creating one at the same time. In order to maintain control of a situation, you must teach yourself to *respond*. When you do, you will experience a tremendous shift in the outcome. Things will be so much easier, and you will get a positive response from those who have had to deal with your reactions in the past.

Perhaps the best part is that you will no longer feel the stress and loss of energy that was caused by your previous behaviors. When dialogues in relationships and life go smoothly, tasks are accomplished faster, feelings aren't hurt, and you have extra time to do things that will make you feel better, rather than hurt yourself and someone you care for or work with.

In addition, simple, everyday interactions and conversations go better. You will also feel a difference in how you are perceived; people will start to get you rather than get *to* you. All you have to do to achieve this earthly state of nirvana is to think before you speak. Simply checking in with yourself and asking, "Am I responding or just reacting?" is the easiest way to change your behavior from destructive to constructive.

It may take a little practice, but discuss the process with someone you trust or love, for he or she may want to help or participate in some fashion. This way you can assist each other in containing the fallout from reactions and molding them into appropriate responses. If the two of you agree, you can create a signal or phrase that allows the person who may be in reaction mode to shift, and give him or her the space to change direction without letting it affect your conversation or relationship. Having a safe method for change will help it happen sooner rather than later.

So right now, take a moment and think about how you would feel if the other person really understood you. That warm feeling inside you, that's the result of choosing to respond rather than react.

28. The Healing Power of Humor

*If we could be twice young and twice old
we could correct all our mistakes.*
—Euripedes

Research shows that laughing every day builds your self-esteem and can add up to eight years to your life. Who knew that having a good guffaw was as healthy as eating broccoli?

Actually, this knowledge has been around for quite a while. Remember Norman Cousins, the author of *Anatomy of an Illness*, who laughed himself well by watching old Three Stooges and Marx Brothers movies? His experience gave him the confidence he needed to create the study of psycho-immunology, which is about how your thinking affects your health. Since his groundbreaking work, a number of theories have developed around the therapeutic power of laughter and humor and its use in counseling and medicine.

I encourage my clients to use humor when they have difficulty dealing with their kids, as well as when they are intensely looking into and perhaps doubting themselves. It's truly one of the most underutilized tools we have as human beings. If more people were able to laugh at themselves, sales of antidepressants would drop dramatically, along with divorce and suicide rates.

Having a sense of humor has a strong positive effect on relationships. When a couple develops the aptitude to see the humor in their behaviors, and even their arguments, their chances of maintaining a successful long-term relationship or life improve dramatically.

When you give someone permission to laugh, you also give him permission to be himself, which is one of the reasons gentle humor can be so therapeutic. We reveal our true emotions only after we feel safe and confident with someone else.

Having the ability to make others laugh is more than a talent; it's a gift for those who get to experience it. Being able to laugh at yourself or the world around you is equally as precious. Laughter will get you through some of the darkest nights and help you cope with the most difficult of days. Look at your life and tell me you can't chuckle at the ironic moments or laugh out loud at some of your self-made bad times.

Sometimes finding things to laugh at and someone to laugh with can be a challenge. You may think you're really funny, but nobody gets you. At other times, life just doesn't give you room or reason to feel a little giddy. In these cases, you need to give yourself a break and take yourself to (or rent) a really good comedy. You can also read something funny or go to a comedy club. Giving yourself a laughter recess will raise your self-confidence, lower your stress level, help you relax, and, at least temporarily, give you time away from your troubles.

Although I believe in a daily dose of yuckin' it up, at least once a week is mandatory to maintain your sense of self-worth. So, check out the funnies or watch some *I Love Lucy* reruns. Whatever makes you giggle is just what this doctor is ordering.

29. Smell the Roses—*Right Now!*

You'll find as you grow older that you weren't born such a great while ago after all. The time shortens up.
—William Dean Howells

"Living in overwhelm" is the norm for most families these days. If you don't agree, think about how many times you've rushed out of work so you can pick up the kids in time to get to the store, just so you can jet home to make dinner and then supervise homework while you get ready for the next day.

I don't think it's possible for anyone to be positive or relaxed under this kind of pressure. Luckily, there are many ways to take back control of your time, figure out how to get things done, and still be able to enjoy being human.

If you're still not convinced you need to relax, realize that science tells us that people who don't relax on a regular basis tend to put on weight, have a greater propensity for depression, and have more relationship issues. It all makes sense when you slow down long enough to think about it...but first you need to create the time.

Initially, you might try imagining what it would be like to take a vacation. When most people think about relaxing, they conjure up images of breezy tropical beaches. And funny as it may sound, having those thoughts may be more calming than actually taking a vacation! Just imagining that you are hanging out at your favorite beach for a couple of minutes will soothe your nerves and lower your brain waves, pulse, and blood pressure. And you don't have to go through airport security to get there.

If life is too hectic, you may want to reevaluate whether you're getting out of it as much as you're putting in. Whether you're in your upwardly mobile years or are struggling to survive, slowing down a little probably won't affect your income or goals as much as you might fear.

I know many successful people who manage to have great careers and take time off. Even if it's only for a few hours or 10 minutes here and there, it can really add to the quality of your life.

You may not think it's possible to find more time for yourself. The key is to make it a priority. Living a balanced emotional life requires at least a little downtime on a regular basis. If you don't relax from time to time, the prospect isn't pretty.

People do die from stress and overwork, but that's not as sad as never really living because you won't take the time to smell a rose or two. All you have to do is make it a point to seize a few moments to enjoy the sunset, the music of a songbird, or the smile on a child's face. It may not be a spa day, but it will make your life longer and a tad bit sweeter.

30. Mental Rehearsal

See it, then you'll believe it.
—Walt Disney

Anyone who has won a game, been promoted, or succeeded at her chosen field spent many hours rehearsing, some of it physical and some of it mental.

There are as many ways to rehearse as there are things to rehearse for. There is always a time to rehearse, even if you don't think you have it. Mental rehearsal is also very valuable, and the upside is that you can mentally rehearse while you are eating your breakfast or driving to an event. What works for you may not work for someone else, but what works for everyone who wants to improve in any area of their lives is some form of regular rehearsal.

There is also rehearsal in the doing. By just doing the thing you want to get better at, you are rehearsing. Any improvement gives you the confidence you need to take on the next project and the one after that. Each time you may be rehearsing for something slightly different, perhaps larger and more complicated. The confidence you gain from all your hard work will continue to serve you. The payoff comes when you realize that you have rehearsed so well you can, for example, give a speech at a moment's notice.

Wouldn't it be great to have that kind of self-assurance? The truth is that those who spend time rehearsing have the confidence to step up to the plate when the opportunity arises.

I'm a big believer in mental rehearsal. Astronauts and Olympic athletes engage in it on a regular basis. Most successful performers and artists also use some form of mental rehearsal. Some call it visualization, or its medical name: clinical guided imagery. No matter what they call it, those who use some kind of mental rehearsal to refine their talents give themselves the greatest opportunity to excel.

It's the combination of mental, physical, and emotional rehearsal that gives you the confidence to compete at the highest level. Go for it.

31. Straighten Up and Feel Right

A clean desk is a sign of a sick mind.
—Albert Einstein

I interviewed organization guru Peter Walsh on my radio show, and just before we went on the air, KCLU general manager Mary Olson told him that, although her desk was a total mess, she knew where everything was. Peter responded by saying, "That statement has made me a wealthy man." And I totally get it.

I have castigated myself far too many times because I couldn't find on my desk a piece (perhaps just a scrap) of paper on which I had written something very important. When this happens my confidence level drops and my anxiety peaks. It is always an uncomfortable experience. Still, keeping the damn thing continually organized is challenging, and I know I'm not alone.

I actually think that organizing your desk from time to time is good therapy. In addition, it lets you know where everything is, and that will reduce the chance of having a minor meltdown when you have to find that piece of paper in a hurry.

For me it doesn't happen on a regular basis; I wait until I can't see the top of my desk because of all the piles of files before I embark on this quest that Ulysses would have second thoughts about.

Once the task is completed, I feel a greater sense of satisfaction. Useless papers have been shredded, expired coupons have been tossed, and there is a sense of order that makes me feel more confident.

It may be a small thing, but, when you put enough of the little things together, you create a big, positive thing. Give it a try! Not only will you feel better about yourself, but you will also find a few things you thought went to that place where all the single socks go.

32. Find Your Inner Geek

Confidence is the companion of success.
—Anonymous

The pride one gets from mastering—or, if you're a techno-spazz like me, just getting the basics of—a computer, is very empowering. These machines can make us crazy (even though they were supposed to make our lives easier). In addition, learning something new builds brain cells and staves off Alzheimer's.

Have you ever wondered why computer malfunctions cause us so much emotional stress? Well, encountering a problem you have no idea how to fix causes anxiety. *Will I get my work done? What have I lost? How much will it cost to fix? Who can I get to help? How long will it take?* And these are just the basic questions.

While you're asking yourself about these, adrenalin and cortisol are coursing through your system, making your body feel differently. From sweating to squirminess, the physical manifestation of angst is very uncomfortable and makes it difficult to concentrate. Even if the problem is solved quickly, going into that momentary panic will take you anywhere from an hour to a day to recover from and get back to your normal level of functioning. And being in that place is not great for your confidence or general well-being.

Knowing how your computer works, and having the ability to dance around a program and make it do what you want it to, can make you feel creative and intelligent. And having the ability to get done what you need to and not encounter any problems allows for greater access to the inner resources and inspiration that we all have.

As you learn something new, you actually stimulate the growth centers of your mind and you create a greater ability to figure out what you need to do next. The confidence of knowing that you can solve a problem, even before you actually encounter it, is very freeing, and allows you to push yourself without feeling pushed.

You can fly though projects like a stunt pilot, doing barrel rolls around your Microsoft Excel spreadsheet, and making Ansel Adams green with envy by your knowledge of Adobe Photoshop. In addition, every time you accomplish a new task, it gives you the opportunity to feel better about yourself. It's a win-win.

If you invest an hour or two a week in a class, many of which are available online, you will master your computer/program of choice in short order. With that ability, you can then create and share your gifts with the world.

Social networking alone can link you up with what's going on in many different parts of the world. By tweeting here or blogging there, you can touch the lives of hundreds of people. Quite simply, knowing your way around the computer connects you to the rest of humanity. And that is a real confidence-builder.

So go get that new laptop or use your kids'; it's time to learn so you can keep up with the rest of the human race.

33. Fix It and Feel It

A comfortable old age is the reward of a well-spent youth. Instead of its bringing sad and melancholy prospects of decay, it should give us hopes of eternal youth in a better world.
—R. Palmer

These days, being able to save a few bucks by "doing it yourself" has become the norm for many of us. Personally, I do not possess any mechanical skills whatsoever, but I can still putter, and upon occasion actually make a repair—or at the very least, move something around and pull a weed or two. The funny thing is that, even though I am a totally lame handyman, every time I put out a little energy into my environment, even if I'm not completely successful at the task, I actually feel better about myself and life in general.

Even though you may not have talent in certain areas, it doesn't mean you can't develop at least a rudimentary skill set. We all have parts of ourselves that don't meet our own expectations, but we also possess the ability to put our personal issues aside for a time in order to accomplish something positive. Think about it: Don't you feel better when you're moving in a forward direction? Most everyone does; it's part of being human. Another part of our humanness is that we enjoy positive emotions, even if the path to feeling them requires painting the living room or fixing a broken whatchamacallit.

Before beginning your project, especially if it's something that you are unfamiliar with, it's always best to consider it from different angles. Walk around it like a lion stalking its prey, look at the nooks and crannies, read the instructions (if you have any), and, if you can, get someone else to help you. Even if he is just handing you parts, having another person with you gives you that all-important moral support.

There is also merit to the idea that even if you think you may never need to know how to do something, such as changing a tire, there *will* come a time when you will have to do it. Even though you have Auto Club or some other service, your car is new, or you never leave town, you need to know how to do this. And it is far better to practice it one time in your driveway than to have to do it on a seedy side street in the middle of the night.

Most of us don't have to look for things we need to learn how to do; we face them every day. But being proactive can save you time, money, and a ton of grief. In addition, once you have a process for tackling tasks outside of your "job description," your life will be easier because you will be confident that you can deal with new and challenging situations.

34. Picture This

Don't let life discourage you; everyone who got where he is had to begin where he was.
—Richard L. Evans

Whether on the computer or in albums, reviewing your history (or herstory) is a great way of seeing where you've been and how you've evolved throughout the years. Looking at old photos can give you a good perspective on how far you have come.

Perhaps you were once a shy underachiever or struggled in school, and now you are in management or created your own business (or maybe both). Somehow, you must have developed self-confidence and a skill set or two along the way.

By reviewing your personal and family history, you may be able to see the significant events or a pattern that led you to breakthrough moments or actions. We all connect with our pasts, and even our sad memories are of times when we have grown and changed. Photos of days gone by will remind you of who you are, and give you a slightly different perspective on where you may want to go.

It also helps you organize your sense of self. Perhaps you used to be depressed or anxious. There may have been periods of which you have no pictures, and it can be enlightening to think about why you didn't bring a camera or didn't want pictures taken. Some families were maybe unable to afford to take pictures; others may have been too busy or distracted. And sadly, a few perhaps chose not to capture the memories because they didn't like something about the people or places.

So even the blank spots have depth, and can add to your understanding of how to be your best self. Taking a few hours every now and then to look at your old self and those who loved you can't help but make you feel more confident about yourself.

35. Keeping a Confidence Journal

You have to expect things of yourself
before you can do them.
—Michael Jordan

Keeping a confidence journal works. The process is elegant in its simplicity: Just write down five things you feel confident about. Doing it on a daily basis changes the way you think and feel. The best time for it is just before bed because the confident thoughts will flow into your subconscious as you sleep. Not only will you awake a bit more confident, but you will also be less stressed and happier.

I know this seems too easy to do any good, but it really works, especially when times are tough. Think about it: If your mind is constantly struggling with your personal situation, or that of the world, the thoughts become overwhelming, and it can be very difficult to find a way out of your troubles.

By utilizing the confidence journal technique, positive thoughts and emotions worm their way into your psyche and slowly but surely change the way you look at, and work with, the people and problems around you. If your attitude is negative, it's very hard to feel good about yourself or your circumstances. When you don't feel good about life, it becomes much more challenging to find a way out. This journaling process can help you find your way to greater peace of mind and additional success.

If all you can see is the worst, changing what you feel internally, even for a few moments, changes your brain chemistry and opens the door to positive thoughts and actions.

As Michael Jordan said, you have to *expect* things of yourself first. Keeping a confidence journal helps to program your mind and creates the room and motivation to achieve those expectations. It's a simple process, and the best time to start is right now.

36. The World Is Your Ally

We all need to see the universe as friendly.
—Albert Einstein

Believing that life is on your side eliminates the fear that the world is out to get you. It also increases your confidence because you won't be looking for the other shoe to drop. Making friends with life allows you to enjoy playing with it, as well as being a player in it.

I know that sometimes life is not easy or fair—for any of us. But if you act as though you are living or working in a war zone, the results of your efforts will end up looking like a bombed-out building. So if you don't want to end up as an empty shell, you need to make a major attitude shift.

The world does not punish us; we are far too good at doing that to ourselves to need any additional assistance. Just living in that type of fear is like putting a tourniquet on your confidence and creativity. We all experience disasters in our lives, but that doesn't mean our lives are disastrous.

Everyone is capable of being pessimistic, but when it becomes a lifestyle you must make some changes in order to move forward. To break this negative cycle, you first have to realize that you may be a little more of an Eeyore than a Tigger, and start to accentuate the positive. That realization alone is a confidence-builder, and every action you take in that direction just makes you stronger.

Things go badly, and then they get better. Recessions end, people find new jobs and relationships—life goes on. If you approach it with just a little confidence and positivity, you will get so much more from the experience. I see life as a limited window of opportunity and choose not to spend much time dwelling on what didn't work. Instead I do what I learned from Dr. Einstein: I see that the world is truly on my side. When something doesn't work out the way I want it to, I truly believe that I simply need to focus in another direction.

If you look at your life, I believe you will see that almost everything you have done, from sports to business to babies, has added to your experience and knowledge. And all that energy gets recycled. Even if you never achieved your dream of being a rock star, that time you spent on stage or in front of the mirror pretending your hairbrush was a microphone actually made you a better communicator.

All of your experiences, good and bad, work together to make you who you are. Even though we may not completely understand why some things don't go right, good things eventually arise from our efforts. Trusting that the world is friendly can only serve you and help you be more confident.

37. Monitor Your Thinking

Sooner or later, those who win are those who think they can.
—Richard Bach

Of the gazillion thoughts we have a day, research has determined that **80** percent are negative. Science also tells us that we remember the negative because doing so was hardwired into our DNA; we had to remember where the tar pits were so we wouldn't fall into them. Times are different now, and our thinking process has to evolve as well.

It doesn't take a rocket scientist or even a "shrink" to realize that negative thoughts will produce downer days. The challenge for those of us who want to keep our thinking as positive as possible is to stop those massive quantities of bad vibes from entering our brains.

As many now know, the first step is to recognize that you have negative thoughts. Some people can catch themselves in the moment, and for others it may take an evaluation that occurs at the end of the day. Either way, looking at your thoughts and seeing the positive-to-negative ratio will be an enlightening experience.

If you'd like to remove all your negative thoughts, sorry, it's not going to happen. I don't believe that it's realistic to think that you can go through life without ever having thoughts you would consider unpleasant. You can, however, lighten up your thinking process considerably, and with very little effort.

After you have spent a week looking at how your mind works, you can then begin to take the uncomfortable thoughts and tell them to go away, one by one, as they come up. Yes, I know this sounds almost silly, but it works. When a negative thought comes up you can mentally stop it. Give it a try, and if you can do it once, you can do it again.

There are additional methods; one business colleague has given his negative inner voice a name, "Boris," and says that when he has a negative thought, he tells Boris to go to his room and the thought dissipates. When a student of mine catches himself feeling bad vibes, he pictures a beautiful forest in his mind's eye, and that takes away the disturbing emotions and thoughts.

Meditation, visualization, and self-hypnosis are other tools that can assist you in this very doable task. Once you have mastered the art of stopping negative thoughts in their tracks, you will be surprised to see that, after you have engaged in the exercise for several weeks, you have substantially less of them.

This isn't some New Age woo-woo thinking. It is an established, studied, and tested method for getting and keeping your thinking process on the positive track. The hardest part is getting started, so now that you've finished reading this, give it a try. It may be a little awkward at first, but most things worth doing take a little practice and patience.

Monitoring your thinking, so you can change from a negative thinker to a positive one, is a great tool to help you build your self-confidence.

38. Up-Level Your Support Structure

Most of us, swimming against the tides of trouble the world knows nothing about, need only a bit of praise or encouragement—and we will make the goal.

—Jerome Fleishman

Support groups have been around long before psychotherapy. Medicine men would gather together and share their latest tools, the women of ancient tribes looked after one another and the children, and individuals were allowed to seek council from the chief when required. If you don't have friends, family, or coworkers who support you emotionally, join a group or form one of your own.

In this case, the latter may actually be easier than the former; groups already in existence require that you mold yourself to their belief structure, and this can totally put some people off. In addition, finding a group that supports your exact needs may be difficult, so starting your own, even somewhat casually, can give you a huge advantage in life and business.

I have written about the benefits and magic of Mastermind Groups in *Emotional Fitness at Work*. These high-level gatherings are not for those in need of a 12-step program; they are for individuals who know they are good, but want to achieve some greatness. Leaders and those who are developing their careers can learn from their peers. Most find that they don't have to reinvent the wheel, as the other members of the group may well have dealt with similar issues, and their experience and advice is priceless.

The other component one gets from groups is emotional support. The old saying that "It's lonely at the top" makes sense to anyone who has been there. As a leader you can't go crying on your VP's shoulder and expect to maintain respect, but it is imperative that you let your feelings out. We all get overwhelmed, and having a place to release frustration or just vent is something we all need to do every now and then. Having a safe place to do this makes it so much easier.

Group or even private therapy is also very helpful, but you may want to integrate emotions and business in your conversation, so you have to find a counselor or group that wants the same things—again, not all that easy, so let's look at how to put your own together.

My friend Brad Oberwager, CEO of Sundria Corporation, has been aware and/or part of a support group for CEOs since he was a kid. His dad was a member of YPO (the Young Presidents Organization), and through sharing that experience he started a group with classmates at the Wharton Business School, and remains in regular contact with them today. He is also a member of the Young Entrepreneurs Organization.

He credits these groups as part of the reason he is at the top of his game, and even in a down economy, his business is growing. By putting together his own group and joining one that has been around for a few decades, he has the best of both worlds, and information that couldn't be gleaned from 20 years of graduate school.

So get out your old phone books, look around at the people you work well with, and make some calls to those who have something you want to learn. Chances are they will like the idea and join you for a meeting, and then you can all see if you'd like it to continue.

The business and emotional support one can get from these experiences is not just a confidence-builder; it is a pathway to personal and financial success.

39. Feel the Love

The hunger for love is much more difficult
to remove than the hunger for bread.
—Mother Teresa

Perhaps nothing will make a person feel better about himself and build self-confidence than being loved by someone he admires. You don't have to be in a romantic relationship with the person; what I'm talking about is unconditional love, and that can come from anywhere.

But it can be a challenge to let it in, especially if you are independent or have been hurt in the past. Don't let a past mishap shut you down to an emotion that can take you to the next level in your life.

If you never had a loving family, it's more difficult to build healthy self-esteem. Appropriate affection from another person may be the magic touch you need to actually believe that you are lovable. When someone you admire gives her heart to you, it makes you feel cherished, and in turn you learn to love yourself.

I know a number of people who were only able to develop self-love after someone who made them feel worthwhile came into their lives. For many, this love blossomed into a healthy and lifelong relationship. For others, it was an experience that put them on a path to finding their true purpose in life.

In many support groups one of the things that helps a person to recover is the fact that the group loves the individual until he or can love himself. This is also one of the ways in which therapy helps individuals to heal from depression, loss, and addiction.

On the other hand, we all know people who are in love with themselves (they're called narcissists). When someone is totally self-absorbed, she may not have room in her heart to care for another human being. When looks, power, or charisma begin to fade, many people with this issue find themselves very depressed and very alone.

If you put yourself before all others and ignore the needs and feelings of those closest to you, you'd better get a grip and change your behavior before your loved ones take a hike. It's very difficult to keep giving love to someone who seldom or never returns it.

For those people who are still struggling with loving themselves, getting reassurance and support from a loving partner is very important in the healing process. Reminding someone who is struggling with self-acceptance that he deserves to be loved is a true gift from the heart.

If you have to continually ask your partner if she loves you, or if your partner is never able to take in the love you have to share, both of you may want to seek some additional support. If you let the pattern continue, your relationship will not have the strength or ability to grow.

Trusting that you are loved may be difficult for someone who has suffered a trauma or significant loss. For those people I suggest patience and persistence. I believe that the heart only has so much room, and if it's filled with hurt there is less room for love. Love actually pushes out the sadness in our hearts, so by letting it in you not only get to feel the wonderful gift of being loved by another, but you also get to release some old pain you may be holding on to.

Remember the story of the princess and the frog? We can all turn into someone charming (and confident) when we let ourselves be loved.

40. Shape Up

Those who think they have not time for bodily exercise
will sooner or later have to find time for illness.
—Edward Stanley

If you are healthy, you have the confidence to accomplish anything. If you are not, mere survival can be a challenge. Being fit is very important to your self-esteem and your physical well-being. Exercise is your easiest, most accessible, and cheapest form of antidepressant. So don't just sit there and read about how good it is for your psyche as well as your body— get up and get moving.

I remember as a child how my father's cigar-smoking buddy would say, in a smoker's throaty voice, "Kid, ya ain't got your health, ya ain't got nothing." At the time, it just seemed gross. Now, a few decades (and a couple of "procedures") later, I realize that, though he didn't take his own advice, he was totally right. Being healthy, and helping those you love do the same, is one of the most important pieces of a confident and fulfilling life.

With the epidemic of obesity, and all the press about how living a healthy lifestyle not only lengthens your life, but also makes you a better person in so many ways, I find it remarkable that so few people take good enough care of themselves. I know a number of folks who take better care of their animals than they do of themselves. I love my pets deeply, and I know if I am unable to use the can opener, they will starve, so I have to be healthy to care for them.

When we are out of shape or our health is poor, the mere basics of life are overwhelming. Some people who have to deal with chronic or even life-threatening illness get more exercise than those who are well but lazy. Finally realizing that without your physical health your situation will not improve anytime soon, and your dreams may never be realized, does inspire most people to get moving. You have to keep the vehicle that propels your thoughts and ideas humming.

I remember watching a woman who, in her later years, began exercising. I passed her almost every day walking slowly up the hill in our neighborhood. When she first started she was overweight, didn't smile, and was wearing very unflattering sweats. After several months I noticed that she had lost a bunch of weight, her hair shone and skin glowed, and she was wearing some very flashy spandex running pants and a skimpy top. She looked great. I actually pulled over and told her that I kinda watched her get into shape and asked her how she felt. She responded, "I finally feel good about myself."

That was enough to get me on the program, and I hope this is enough to do the same for you. Dropping that extra weight and feeling strong is going to improve your self-confidence no matter what stage of life you are in.

41. Trust Your Gut

The body never lies.
—Martha Graham

Scientists have discovered that there is actually a type of thinking function that goes on in our digestive tracts: It's called the enteric nervous system.

We've all had "gut feelings" or intuitions, but many people don't realize how much they depend on them. Intuition isn't about picking lottery numbers; it is simply another form of knowledge that should be considered. It is a way to listen to what's going on inside yourself, and it can help you deal with questions of all types, as well as depression and anxiety.

If you dispute the value of your own intuition, ask yourself how many times you have had a thought, not listened to it, and later wished you had. The truth is that your body knows as much as your mind—if not more, in some cases. The trick is to learn how to tune in to that very helpful part of your being, and step one is to trust that it's real.

Although following your gut feelings can be a little scary at first (and you might wonder if people will start looking at you as though you're from another planet), doing so can be really helpful in navigating life's constant changes, and it is usually harmless.

Using your intuition can open you up to new ideas or help you find answers to questions you may have. The intuitive process requires that you are at least somewhat relaxed and in touch with your feelings, not letting your emotions control you.

The best way to begin is to take a deep breath, close your eyes, and concentrate on what's going on within you. Sometimes it helps to focus on your breath. It sounds simple, and it is, once you've practiced it several dozen times. Don't get frustrated if you feel as though you're doing it all wrong and not getting anywhere. Be gentle with yourself and try this technique as often as possible. We all have intuition. It's a matter of tapping in.

Trust those butterflies in your stomach, and your dreams to be the best or to create the next Facebook. Listen to that little voice inside you that says "yes." These are all ways our intuition manifests within us. It's not something you program like a computer. It's more a process of building a muscle within your psyche. Just slow down and let it flow naturally.

Artists, writers, and musicians all use their intuition to create. Parents use it to keep their children safe, and billions of people make decisions based on their gut feelings every day. Trusting your intuition is a great tool for making your life and your relationships work better.

42. Celebrate Small Victories

The good Lord gave you a body that can stand most anything. It's your mind you have to convince.
—Vince Lombardi

The common thinking is: To become successful, you need to be confident first—not so, for millions of people the opposite has proven true. This is because creating success in one arena of your life, even a very small one, affects every other area as well.

Small victories, as I like to call them, can be anything from finding a great parking space or buying a lottery ticket and winning $10. The trick to turning these micro-successes into confidence is that you have to take them in. What I mean by that is you need to fully experience the emotions associated with success.

By allowing yourself to feel successful, you are training your brain cells and giving them the most addictive force in nature: intermittent positive reinforcement. Every time you give your psyche something it feels good about, it will gravitate to that feeling as often as possible. If you celebrate successes throughout the day, no matter how small, you can't help but increase your desire to want more and, along with it, your self-worth.

Little things that may seem insignificant, or even a waste of time, can help you reach your biggest goals. For example, honestly knowing in your own mind that the presentation you just gave was a home run, even though there were only four people in the room, helps you train your brain to want the experience of success to occur again. Consciously or unconsciously, you will make it happen.

By acknowledging to yourself that you achieved something positive, you internally imprint it on your brain. Think of it as being saved in your mind's hard drive. It's in there, just like that document on your computer you've been searching for. Once you find it, you will always know where it is and how to open it.

Similarly, once you know how to be successful or what it feels like to be confident, you can access the programming for those emotions because they are stored in your brain, and you will remember how to find them.

For some who are struggling, even the idea of a tiny victory seems out of reach—if you can't even get out of bed in the morning, you aren't going to feel the success of taking a walk or planting some posies. So you have to pare down your goals appropriately. See getting out of bed and into the shower as a tiny victory and sitting in your backyard reading the paper as another. Push yourself to do a tiny bit more each day and soon you'll be taking that walk, and life won't seem impossible.

Success happens. It happens to everyone every day. Seeing it manifest within our lives may just be a matter of opening up our eyes and giving ourselves a pat on the back. Building your own confidence from your own success is the purest form of self-esteem.

43. The Confidence Circle

You can determine how confident people are by listening to what they don't say about themselves.
—Brian G. Jett

Sometimes you can gain personal empowerment from group exercises, and there are a few that can do wonders for your self-confidence. Most are fun games, and some can really be impactful in a positive and upbeat way. This particular exercise requires five to 10 people:

One person sits in the middle while the others gather together in a circle around him (hand-holding is not required). Each person sitting in the outside circle will tell the person within it several things that they like about him.

When everyone in the circle has finished, the person in the middle shares what he remembers hearing, and then the next person in the group changes places with him.

There should be a scribe taking notes or videotaping the exercise so everyone can see what they got and what they missed. Do this part at the end of the exercise after everyone has experienced being the recipient.

The trick is this: The things you remember and are able to repeat are the things you believe about yourself. We know this because you were able to take them in and identify with them. It may surprise you that things were said that you didn't think others saw in you. This process helps you reinforce the confidence you already have, and perhaps build some in areas in which you'd like to have more.

The compliments you were unable to retain are areas where you don't feel as though you're at the top of your game or you feel you don't deserve the praise. It is important to note that these positive statements came from people who see you in ways you may not be able to see yourself. Getting an outside perspective is a valuable tool when it comes to being your best and building your confidence.

In the spirit of total honesty, the first time I did this exercise, the only compliment I could remember was that several people said I was funny. I was very young, but I did realize that I should have been able to absorb more positive input, and this exercise inspired me to do just that. I learned to listen to the good things people said about and to me. Although I am still surprised when someone compliments my writing or my speaking, and even though I may not see the same good things, I work to take the compliments in. I believe that doing so makes me better at what I do, and of course raises my self-esteem.

Try this exercise several times throughout the course of a year and you will increase your self-confidence.

44. Writing Heals

One of the greatest moments in anybody's developing experience is when he no longer tries to hide from himself but determines to get acquainted with himself as he really is.
—Norman Vincent Peale

I love going to see Lyle Lovett, a very self-confident guy and one of my favorite musicians. I've been a fan since before Julia Roberts because I really respect his creativity. At one concert he told a few stories, as artists who have been around for a decade or two like to do, and with his droll sense of humor, well, all I can say is that I enjoyed the patter as much as the tunes.

One thing he shared with the audience that stuck with me, and that I heard others mention as we left the show, was, "For anyone who writes, writing is therapy. Don't let anyone tell you different." Not a hard sell for me; I totally get it, and so do a lot of other people.

Writing is a great healer and confidence-builder. You can let out your feelings—good, bad, or indifferent— and actually feel a weight being lifted off of you. Whether it's writing music, books, a journal, or a column, the process of putting your thoughts down on paper can be an amazing release as well as a way of seeing your own growth.

If your words and thoughts are sad, writing can be a cathartic experience, such that you cry as you write—and we all need a good cry every now and then. Emotional outpourings can also contain laughter as well as tears, and still be deep and healing.

There is a great scene in the film *Something's Gotta Give* in which the successful Diane Keaton is writing a play that is about her relationship with Jack Nicholson, and, as she puts the finishing touches on it, she weeps as she types, and also laughs at her own feelings and experience. As she shares her broken heart with the world she realizes that others would relate to the joy and pain of love and life. She also feels confident that her play is going to be a success.

If you keep those emotions bottled up inside, eventually something is going to give and you will emotionally pop or perhaps become depressed, and your confidence will surely take a hit. Writing on a regular basis is a great way to get out insecure feelings and free up your heart and head to move forward. Yes, it can be good therapy, even if you didn't plan on it.

There are many ways to engage in the process. These days anyone can share their feelings with the online world by writing a blog—there must be millions of them. You can set one up for free at blogger.com.

What about writing that book or screenplay you've had in your head for the past several years? You don't have to pen another *War and Peace* for this to work for you. A paragraph or two can do wonders.

If you don't care to let a few billion folks into your private life, keeping a personal journal can be a good vehicle to help you get into your feelings and get rid of your pain.

The point here is that writing is a valuable tool for your self-confidence. So put your fingers on the keyboard (or your guitar) and let your heart speak. Whatever the result, you will be better for it.

45. Don't Lower Yourself by Raising Your Voice

Always end the name of your child with a vowel, so that when you yell, the name will carry.
—Bill Cosby

One of the most damaging behaviors in any personal or business relationship is verbal abuse. Quite simply, it makes you look like an insecure bully. The truth is: Self-confident people never need to yell.

Luckily, yelling can be one of the easiest patterns to change. This is one of the cases in which it helps to look into the past and see if anything in your history allowed this bad habit to fester.

Perhaps you came from a home environment where yelling and put-downs were commonplace and accepted as part of the family dynamic. Many people see nothing wrong with it, but that is only because they are not consciously affected by it. Unfortunately, the unconscious effects are significant. Look at what it did to your self-image and confidence level.

People who come from, or live and work in, a verbally abusive environment are less secure than the rest of us. They walk around wondering if they will have a job or their relationship tomorrow—not a great way to live.

Among the strongest tools you have to help eliminate this bad behavior is setting your own example. If you yell, you are giving those around you permission (and lessons) to do the same. If the cycle has been around for a couple of generations, this may be time to make a change. It's not as difficult as you may think.

The first thing you need to do is become aware of the behavior. Catching yourself is a good place to start. Realizing that you actually do occasionally become overbearing will help you stop yourself.

Those who are truly brave and who really want their lives to be better will also give their loved ones (as well as friends and/or coworkers) permission to remind them, when they engage in loud conversations, that yelling isn't something they want to do any longer. It can take a moment to remember why you don't want to be verbally abusive and want to calm yourself down.

Techniques for finding that calm can be as simple as taking a walk, going into your backyard, taking a very deep breath, or just closing your eyes and mentally putting yourself into a better emotional state.

It's hard when you get overheated to stop verbal abuse in its tracks, but the results are worth it. This is a case in which practice makes perfect, and the more times you try to break the pattern, the easier it will be.

Learning to avoid the destructive energy of verbal abuse will make your life better, at home and anywhere else. You will also gain self-respect and confidence because you are dealing with life in an adult manner, and you will get respect from others in return.

So watch yourself and learn to speak in a tone that will make your friends and family welcome your conversations and suggestions. You don't ever need to lower yourself by raising your voice.

46. No Anxiety? Not Possible

*If I have the belief that I can do it, I shall
surely acquire the capacity to do it even if
I may not have it at the beginning.*
—Mahatma Gandhi

People think that they are supposed to live anxiety-free—not so. This is not an existential concept; anxiety is part of the human condition. We all experience it on an almost-daily basis in one form or another, and, in some ways, it can be helpful.

I think it's important to realize that we grow most through meeting the challenges of difficult and painful experiences. Things that once intimidated us, when overcome, contribute to our growth and confidence.

Hey, don't get me wrong, I'd love an anxiety-free existence, but where would we be without worry? It does keep us safe in a number of ways: We avoid stepping off cliffs or (metaphorically speaking) sticking our hand in the lion's mouth, because we know we can get hurt.

Anxiety also serves us in smaller ways by letting us know that something isn't quite right, so we can make the appropriate adjustments. Those little niggling feelings in the back of your brain are a combination of anxiety and intuition trying to get your attention so you can make sure you are safe and heading in the right direction.

The trick here is to learn to use your anxiety in positive ways. The first step in doing that is to see what the payoff of an anxious moment might be for you. Perhaps it's telling you that this assignment isn't quite right for you, or that you really can't afford that new flat-screen television. I think it's wise to at least check out your feelings before you leap.

Another side of the coin is that excitement and anxiety feel exactly the same to our bodies. And it's quite common for people to feel both excited and scared at the same time. Thrill rides at amusement parks (and first dates) give you that feeling, and in these cases, it's perfectly normal, and usually fun.

A number of folks do suffer from Generalized Anxiety Disorder (GAD) or panic attacks, and that's a different story. Most of us don't worry about normal, daily activities on a regular basis. If you do, and it's gone on for six months or more, you really need to get a checkup, correct diagnosis, and treatment.

Anxiety can shake you to your core. Your confidence evaporates, your ability to communicate is hampered, and your thinking process is blinded by fear. Learning how to avoid it, control it, and deal with it appropriately is a skill set that will serve you for the rest of your life.

When anxiety strikes, it helps to remember that you have dealt with similar events before, and that you have the tools to get through this one as well. Sit down (or pull over), take a few deep breaths, and think through the situation. Chances are you will find that the answers you need are already inside your head, and once you calm yourself down a little, you will see them much more clearly.

47. Giving When It Hurts

How wonderful it is that nobody need wait a single moment before starting to improve the world.
—Anne Frank

Helping others reminds you that you are a good person and that you can use what you know in positive ways. The feeling of giving to someone who would benefit from your experience and generosity is priceless. It is also one of the best antidepressants available, because there is a direct connection between giving and feeling good about yourself. The former almost always leads to the latter.

In tough times, giving money to a worthy cause or even volunteering can seem counterproductive. After all, the old saying that "charity begins at home" makes sense when you're struggling to pay your bills or are out of work yourself. Still, many people find ways to give of themselves even more when things are difficult. Those who do simply say, "It makes me feel good."

If you are used to getting up and going to the office every day and are now out of work, maintaining your routine by volunteering can be helpful; you can only send out so many resumes and applications. Yes, you need to be available for interviews, but most places where you can volunteer will understand that you have other things you need to do to survive.

If you are overemployed, or just very busy, giving money will also make you feel better about yourself. I really believe that donating should continue to take place even when you're not raking in the bucks, but in unstable times it can be a little scary to share what you may possibly need in the near future. I understand, but that is also the time when it's most important.

Giving promotes a kind of energy exchange. Several times in my life, when things were not financially great, I continued donating to a few organizations and people that I believed in supporting. Things always turned around, and I know that by continuing to give, I opened up the opportunity to improve my world, which had a direct effect on my life getting better.

I know it sounds a little out there, but it works, and just by giving a little bit to someone in need, you create a different dynamic in your life. You build self-respect because you see that you are directly responsible for making the world, or even just one person's existence, better.

Albert Einstein said, "It is every man's obligation to put back into the world at least the equivalent of what he takes out of it." Yes, things are tougher out there right now, but don't let that stop you from engaging in this laudable pursuit. Most of the time, when we give to those in need, it does make a constructive impact on both the giver and the receiver.

One of the best ways to create success in life is to see a need and fill it. So share your time, talent, or treasure—I promise that it will come back to you in positive ways.

(The film *Pay it Forward* exemplifies this behavior; if you haven't seen it, put it on your DVD rental list.)

48. How Others Have Built Confidence

It's lack of faith that makes people afraid of meeting challenges, and I believe in myself.
—Muhammad Ali

One of the best ways to build self-confidence is to look at how someone you respect did it. Examining how people we admire have raised their confidence level and changed their circumstances can teach us what we need to do to enhance our own lives.

To begin this process, first consider the people you know and admire. Most successful individuals relish the opportunity to share their knowledge, and how they got to where they are, with someone who respects them.

After she has agreed to meet with you, and I believe that it is best to do this in person if at all possible, prepare a list of questions. This will help you focus your time and not waste your advisor's. It will also bring up other questions that you may not know you have until you've asked a few.

This process alone is a confidence-builder, and the meeting may just be the cherry on top. Knowing that someone you respect will take his or her time to talk with you is bound to make you feel good about yourself.

Perhaps the person you'd most like to talk to is someone you don't know personally, but only through his work. Great minds and individuals are far more accessible than you might think. I have had very little trouble connecting with well-known people whom I honestly believed wouldn't give me the time of day. As it turns out, almost everyone I have contacted with a question has gotten back to me, and I have even developed professional relationships with a number of them—all because I took the risk of sending an e-mail or making a call.

If I had never risked asking for some information (or an interview) I never would have gotten to know most of the esteemed professionals who endorsed this book. I also grew from our conversations. The truth is that whenever you do your job right, everyone involved grows.

I do understand that talking to someone you don't know is scary, but isn't that the point? Getting past that fear will allow you to open up some additional doors while also reinforcing your confidence.

Once you start talking, just let the conversation go where it wants to, and allow the person you are talking with to ask you a few questions as well. The give and take will make your talk flow more easily, and again, one question usually leads to another, plus a few different answers that perhaps you weren't expecting.

I also think a lot can be gained by reading biographies of famous people. Confidence (and the wisdom of how to attain it) is shared with eloquence and humor by both Ben Franklin and Mark Twain. Different insights to forging self-confidence and building a successful life are also shared by Warren Buffett and Tony Robbins, to name a few others.

The information you need is out there, and all you have to do to get it is make a call, send a note, or pick up a book. The next step is in your hands.

49. Mean People Suck

Confidence...thrives on honesty, on honor, on the sacredness of obligations, on faithful protection and on unselfish performance. Without them it cannot live.
—Franklin D. Roosevelt

On several occasions my desire to see the good in people has blinded me to the arguably brutal negativity that some misdirected souls feel entitled to inflict on others. Perhaps the greatest betrayal is when someone we trust is mean to us. It messes with our esteem as well as our trust in that person, and it can affect other relationships as well.

Some people use meanness to get their way. Sometimes it's a pouty mean, the kind we use when we are children to give a voice to our powerlessness. At other times meanness can be an equalizer, giving someone the perception that she can protect herself from an emotional terrorist. People who try to vanquish negativity in this manner are usually outmatched. It's also hard to keep mean energy inside you if you are not really a mean person. But, most unfortunately, truly mean people do exist.

Some overtly aggressive humans act out in ways that they sense will make their victims cower. Most normal people who are being treated this way will submit to almost anything to get rid of the pain and anxiety. Mean people also enjoy the feeling of power their behavior gives them. For them, being mean is an addiction, and the meanness becomes something they try to keep burning inside themselves. They must be unaware of how this type of personality will eventually destroy any relationship or crumb of love that might have come their way.

It seems that there is more meanness today than in the past. I witness rudeness to service people who are doing their jobs with a smile, teenagers insulting each other as though it were an art form, and separated couples trying fruitlessly to seek revenge through the courts and their children. Everyone has to win, and most who get into this pattern will stop at nothing. When this happens, everyone ends up losing.

If you have to deal with a mean person on a regular basis, here are three things you can do to be more confident in that situation.

1. Get support. Telling someone what you are going through will help give you a place to put your pain and perhaps give you some perspective. Whether this is a one-time event or an ongoing tragedy, the benefit of sharing your feelings will help to heal them.

2. Realize you have a choice. If you've been brought up around mean people, being around someone who understands and is sensitive can be an eye-opener. Not everyone behaves in a toxic manner. Choose to associate with people who are kind.

3. Get out of the way. Most people leave their jobs because they don't get along with their bosses. It's okay to leave or to end something if you are being abused. This goes for personal as well as professional relationships.

I don't think I've ever seen someone respond positively to meanness. Meanness is a poor tactic used by the insecure, and it never works in the end. If you are mean, give it up. Like the song says, "Mean people suck."

50. No One Has All the Answers

No one person has all the answers.
—Peter Charles Goldsmith

My dad was the first person to teach me about confidence. One of the things he stressed was that he (or I) couldn't possibly know it all. He believed in getting feedback from those around him in order to make the best decision for everyone involved. Having good people to go to can't help but make you more self-confident. With that in mind, I decided to ask some of my favorite authors what they learned from their dads. Here's what they told me.

- "My father taught me to be a man of my word. He lived by example. Even though there were many times we were in conflict as I grew up, I have to hand it to him, he always kept his word. He would say, 'Don't give your word unless you intend to keep it,' and 'A man's word is like a contract.'" —Stephen Trudeau, Psy.D., co-host of "Emotional Fitness" (KCLU/NPR)

- "When my father was dying, he requested that his caregiver read him chapters from my first book, *Second Sight*, which was about my life. That my father wanted to hear this in his last hours and minutes touched my heart and taught me about the poignancy of father-daughter love. I still feel his love in my life today." —Judith Orloff, MD, author of *Emotional Freedom*

- "My dad's father died when he was 12, of tuberculosis. He had no life insurance, and his wife and six children were in deep trouble. They had a difficult time surviving, and yet many years later, I heard my dad say, 'My father dying when I was 12 was one of the best things that ever happened to me.' I asked him how he could say that, and he answered, 'It taught me about what was important in life and that money was to help make people's lives easier.'" —Bernie Siegel, MD, author of *Faith, Hope & Healing*

- "My dad taught me the value of commitment. He was committed to his vocation, his faith, and his wife—my mother. He never talked much about any of these, but his example greatly influenced my life. I believe that commitment is the glue that holds life together, especially through the tough times." —Gary D. Chapman, author of *The Five Love Languages*

- "My father is a role model for me: He has taught me tolerance and empathy, but also perseverance and, above all, to apply yourself to every situation. In this way, he has prepared me for the complexities of life, and I owe him a great debt." —Susan Shapiro Barash, author of *Second Wives*

- "I learned from my father to never trust anyone who begins a sentence with the words 'to tell you the truth,' and that the greatest gift a father can give to his children is to love their mother." —Allan J. Hamilton, MD, author of *The Scalpel and the Soul*

- "One of the most precious gifts my father gave me was demonstrating that love includes being of service in the world and that attaining worldly success need not require sacrificing ethics or integrity." —Dr. David Gruder, author of *The New IQ*
- "My father was a role model who taught me to be ready to give my all to others. One day he was up on our roof repairing shingles when our neighbor accidently caught on fire. My dad jumped off the roof, pushed his neighbor down and rolled him over to help put out the flames!" —Dr. Diana Kirschner, author of *Love in 90 Days*
- "My dad taught me the importance of making a decision and committing to it. He also taught me that you should reassess your decisions on a regular basis and have the courage to admit that it's time to change course. The secret is in the commitment and the follow-through. Never let indecision make the decision for you." —Peter Walsh, author of *It's All Too Much*

Indeed, we have much to learn from our fathers. Even if you're on the outs with your papa, he did teach you a thing or two. No matter what happens, those lessons will always be with you.

51. Things Learned From Mothers

Some mothers are kissing mothers and some are scolding mothers, but it is love just the same, and most mothers kiss and scold together.
—Pearl S. Buck

I've learned a lot from the mothers in my life—my own as well as the mothers of people I've known. I wouldn't be where I am if not for their advice, and I can't tell you how many phone calls and e-mails I have gotten that began with, "My mother sent me this column...." Here are some things that a few of us have learned from our moms.

- "When you are a mother, you are never really alone in your thoughts. A mother always has to think twice, once for herself and once for her child." —Sophia Loren, *Women and Beauty*

- "Your mother was the first woman you ever loved. Never forget that. Her nurturing is love in action, and that speaks louder than words." —Stephan Poulter, PhD, author of *The Mother Factor*

- "Kissing a boo-boo makes it all better. No matter how old you are, you always want your mother to be there for you with chicken soup and a soft voice when you're not feeling well. Remember too that bad days don't last forever. Mom always said that tomorrow would be better." —Margret Goldsmith

- "You can fail because of it, or succeed in spite of it. It all depends on how you choose to deal with the bumps in the road." —Sydney MacEwen, Shelley's daughter

- "My momma cat taught me that not every person you meet is worth rubbing up against, and sometimes it's okay to be a little finicky. It could save you from coughing up a hairball later in life." —Piewackett

- "This is what my mother told me before I came to the USA: You can run 1,000 MPH, but if you don't decide where to go before you'll run in a circle and go nowhere. A goal without a plan is just a wish and we can waste time in wishing. —Fabio Viviani, executive chef (and *Top Chef* fan favorite

- "If things are not going your way, take a couple of hours out, grab a girlfriend or a daughter, and hit a chick flick. It's a surefire way to melt away the blues for a little bit."—Mary Trudeau, Devin's mom

- "We have not come into the world to be numbered; we have been created for a purpose; for great things: to love and be loved." —Mother Teresa

- "If you doubt you can accomplish something, then you can't accomplish it. You have to have confidence in your ability, and then be tough enough to follow through." —Rosalynn Carter

The love we give and get from our mothers is a true experience of life's never-ending circle. No matter what, it's never too late to have a loving relationship with your mother. So what if you've been disconnected for years? The bottom line is, she's still your mom; let her know you're still her kid.

52. From Competition to Envy

As iron is eaten by rust, so are the envious consumed by envy.
—Antisthenes

Sometimes the drive to compete and win, which can be great for helping us move forward in life, can backfire and create difficulty and distress between people who may have been lifelong friends. Understanding the different levels of this force can help us use it to our advantage, and realize when we've crossed a line that can cause us emotional harm. Truly understanding these very different and potentially damaging states of mind will give you the confidence you need to deal with uncomfortable situations when they arise.

Competition. We learn to compete at an early age. Whether we want attention, the biggest piece of cake, or our woobie, we learn that being first usually means getting what we want. It also feels good when we've won a game or gotten a good grade. It's not a bad principle, but when competition leads to anger and trying to get even, things can get ugly. We need to teach our children and ourselves that, though a little competition is good, winning isn't as important as being fair.

Rivalry. Think of rivalry as competition with a dash of antagonism. Friends can be rivals, but generally it's not a "friendly competition." There is a desire on the part of one or both to beat the other out and come away with the prize—and be friends later (but only if I win). It's not a horrible way to relate, but you do miss the bond of true friendship. Reaching your own goals may require some teamwork, so it's best not to alienate those close to you. If a rivalry helps you to be your best, and you can also maintain your relationship, that's great.

Envy. This feeling can best be described as "I want what you've got." It doesn't mean the person who envies doesn't want you to succeed; it's just that they want success, too. Envy can actually propel us to reach new heights, especially when we have been unaware of the possibility. For example, if you never knew there was such a thing as a Pulitzer Prize, you wouldn't miss it.

Jealousy. Gore Vidal said, "It's not enough for me to win, you have to lose," and that is the essence of this most destructive feeling. Jealousy makes us think that there isn't enough to go around, so the other person has to lose or, metaphorically speaking, die. The anxiety and anger it provokes are damaging, so be extra cautious if this is a feeling emerging within you or someone you are close to.

It has been said that awareness of a problem is 50 percent of the cure. Knowing how you and those around you are responding to good things happening in your life will help those good things continue. And when people don't respond appropriately, having the wisdom to deal with those instances takes your confidence to a whole new level.

53. Creative Confidence

*The way to develop self-confidence
is to do the thing you fear.*
—William Jennings Bryan

I have no talent in the visual arts, but I did spend a year in art school just to make sure. I remember the first day of my drawing class. I was well prepared with my butcher paper and my tackle box full of the other tools of the trade—all of which up until this point, I had never touched.

I walked to class, my shoulder-length hair blowing in the Berkeley breeze, and found a spot in the room with good light (actually it was near a window, and I like fresh air). I set up my easel and opened my little box of colors, waiting for the professor to set a vase or some form of still life on the pedestal in the center of the room.

I wasn't paying too much attention when a young woman in a kimono walked to the center of the room, stepped on the platform, and took off her robe. Obviously it got my attention, but it wasn't for the reason you are thinking. I was totally freaked out because I knew that I couldn't draw a person and I was about to fail my first class.

I tried hiding behind my easel, hoping that the professor wouldn't see me pretending to artistically interpret the live model. As luck would have it, he had been standing behind me for five minutes.

"Do we have a problem, young man?" he asked in a totally patronizing tone. I just looked at him, shook my head, and replied, "Where's the bowl of fruit?" He looked down his nose at me, pushed his glasses toward his eyes, and started rummaging through my pristine supply box.

He took out a bottle of India ink, popped off the top, and flamboyantly threw it over his shoulder. He then looked on the floor and found a twig, which he put into the bottle of ink. The professor took out a little note pad from his pocket; I thought he was going to write me up for something. Instead, he ripped out a piece of paper and taped it to my drawing board. He handed me the bottle and twig and said, "Now draw what you see."

That was a very freeing moment for me. I was no longer constricted by having to draw an actual person—after all, how could anyone do that with a twig and some ink on a little scrap of paper? As it turns out, I could.

My professor gave me new tools and removed the restriction of my work having to fit into the same category as the other students. What I created with my little stick and black ink resembled a human form, and I was actually proud of myself. It boosted my confidence.

The experience of thinking I was failing, and then being redirected and encouraged to try it a much different way, was totally empowering. I have now learned to give those opportunities to myself.

54. Resolving Difficult Conversations

Every person is in some way my superior,
in that I can learn from him.
—Ralph Waldo Emerson

The only way to appropriately handle conflict is to actually deal with it. Most people avoid difficult conversations because, quite frankly, they are uncomfortable. Unfortunately, if you avoid dealing with a troublesome situation, you're actually prolonging the agony, and may be creating some resentment. This is where feeling confident about your communication skills, as well as yourself, is imperative.

Here are some tips for easing into and having a successful conversation about a difficult topic.

First, be the one to open the lines of communication and ask for input from the other party to help you best figure out a balanced solution to your issue. Doing so says that you care enough (and are confident enough) to take the risk. In addition it gives you a little extra power because you got the ball rolling. This will also greatly reduce the other person's defensiveness and make him more available to participate.

Once the conversation begins, acknowledge the other person's willingness to talk with you. Thank him for talking with you both at the start and the end. It will make the discussion a team effort and make him feel he has given of himself. It will also make having the next difficult conversation easier because it diminishes defensiveness.

Setting a time limit for the conversation can save you a lot of grief. It's important that you talk, but also that you don't wear each other out. Around 30 minutes to an hour is about the most people can take. If you need to continue the conversation, make an appointment to do so in the next couple of days; that way things aren't left hanging.

Learning to paraphrase each other's comments by telling each other what you heard one another say will let each person know that you really "got" (or didn't get) how each of you are feeling. This may seem a little cumbersome at first, but it works to everyone's benefit by maintaining clarity. It will also make both of you feel confident that the conversation is going in the direction you want it to.

Resolution is all about compromise, and how you get there will determine your level of satisfaction with the outcome. Giving a person what she needs, or wants, is not the same as giving up or giving in. Your attitude here is very important. The goal is to be confident, not cocky, and work toward both of you feeling that you got what you needed and that you can drop any ill feelings that may have arisen.

It can help to make a list of what questions you have and what you'd like the other person to do; having something in writing always makes it easier to remember points and to stay on topic. It also helps you make sure you complete the whole issue rather than just some of its parts.

Be okay with being wrong. Difficult conversations don't always end the way you'd like them to. Sometimes an apology or a change of mind is appropriate. Holding a grudge just because you didn't get everything you thought you wanted will only cause more discord. Confident people don't mind being wrong; in fact, most see it as an opportunity to learn for the next time.

Seeking out and respecting expert advice will help you affirm what you know and help you learn what you don't. Remember that no one person knows everything, so going to different resources is totally appropriate. Asking for a third party to help mediate your conversation if it starts to degrade into an argument is also totally acceptable. If you talk with a coworker, professor, therapist, or expert who defends or rebuts your opinions, take the time to consider what he has to say. You will be wiser for it.

Understanding the emotional component of communication will help you defuse problems much easier. Difficult conversations can bring up lots of feelings; make sure you're speaking from your heart, but don't let your emotions run you. Talk about what you are actually feeling versus what you think the other person is feeling about you. That will help to keep the communication clear and minimize the chance of feelings of guilt or anger.

Once everyone has stated their points and agreements have been made, consolidate the gains and recommit to moving things forward. After you have had the conversation, review what you have decided to do (even if that is only to continue the talking at another time), agree upon the conclusion, and let the other person/people know that you are available for additional talks if wanted. Lastly, don't punish them for bringing up a difficult issue.

Being able to have a successful difficult conversation is one of the most valuable tools you can have to build and maintain your self-confidence. For most people this isn't easy, but with time, willingness, and practice anyone can do it. Getting past the first level of discomfort is key, as is knowing that, once you have gotten your issues on the table, your life will be lighter and brighter.

55. That's the Ticket

Youth is a circumstance you can't do anything about.
The trick is to grow up without getting old.
—Frank Lloyd Wright

Every time I see a good concert or musical, I am on a natural high for at least a week. A few are standouts, but even if the show didn't knock my socks off, it's almost always a pleasant experience that leaves me feeling good about life and myself as well.

I feel good that I thought about going, found great seats, managed to carve out the time, had the money to buy the tickets, and, if the drive went well, had a perfect night. How can a relatively flawless experience that you enjoy to the fullest not make you feel more confident?

Spending an evening enjoying sights and sounds that make me smile is just what I like to do; your idea of a perfect day/night may be completely different, and that is as it should be. The point isn't what you do; it's about getting the gumption to do it.

By the way, the act of stalking Ticketmaster, going online, or calling right as the tickets go on sale and scoring great seats is a confidence-builder in itself.

So often we avoid the things we love by finding excuses such as the cost, the time, and the stress, and those thoughts keep us from even trying. Well, if you never get to do what you like, then really, what's the point of it all? If you are feeling concerned about your survival right now, that's understandable; you have to put first things first, and I get that, but most of us aren't in those kinds of dire straights just yet.

Some people's health issues can keep them from seeking their bliss, but I find that many folks who are dealing with chronic and even terminal illness feel better when they can do something they love, if even for only a few minutes. Some would call it therapy, but I think of it more as just living life while you've got it. I remind myself every day that life is a limited window and we've got to at least try to experience firsthand some of the goodies, rather than just watching others rock out to our favorite bands on MTV.

Participating in your joys has to be a self-confidence builder (unless of course you golf). Doing what you love to do makes every fiber of your being sing, and usually after you have finished, not only do you want to do some more, but you want to do it better. And once you sit front-row center, there ain't no goin' back.

Simply put, doing things that you enjoy helps you feel better about life. We all have things that make us feel good, and that's why we enjoy them. A balanced and successful life occurs when you are able to do what you love and make a living at it.

People who have created their lives in this manner are the most self-confident individuals on the planet. Somehow they put it all together and have built a lifestyle that most other people can only admire. It's not about money; it's about joy, and you can't have that without feeling good about yourself.

Psychologically, doing what you love gives you the feeling that you are part of something bigger than you are. The positivity you feel produces chemicals in your brain such as dopamine that make you feel good about yourself, and that is a necessity for achieving goals and even finding love.

Whether it's the energy of the crowd, the view from a mountaintop, or the feeling of pride you get from creating something artistic, doing things you love lifts your confidence to the next level. Who would have thought that just by having fun you are actually doing something good for yourself?

56. Eliminate Critical Comments

Never bend your head. Always hold it high.
Look the world straight in the face.
—Helen Keller

Saying hurtful things will push anyone away, and if you do it enough, no one will want to connect or communicate with you. At that point, you no longer have an emotional support structure, and self-confidence will be as elusive as a shooting star.

We can all nitpick to the point of making those we work with, and care for, run for the hills or cover their ears and say "La la la..." so they won't hear you. People simply tune out critical comments when they become a way of life.

When you are constantly critiquing, the person getting the so-called benefit of your sage advice may just be acting in a polite manner to get you to stop as soon as possible. Although you are trying to help, you are actually pushing this person away. And when your words are blown off, you will feel that your advice is not respected or accepted. It can't be good for your self-confidence when your message, no matter how correct, is not received.

To avoid this negative cycle, think about your choice of words carefully, and, before you decide whether to tell someone how you feel (or just tell her off), imagine how you would respond. If you'd get tweaked, then so will she. This is a simple thinking process that all too few of us engage in.

Most of the time, when we think we have an idea of how someone could do things better, we feel it's our duty to share our insights with him. But the truth is that, no matter who that person is, he is most likely trying to do his best, and you telling him that it could have been done better will only take the wind out of his sails.

If you really think you can improve someone's life, actions, or work with your input, wait until everyone else is out of the room and say something such as, "I really liked what you had to say, but I don't think everyone got you. I have an idea that may help you, if you'd like to hear it."

By communicating in a way that doesn't make people feel judged or put down, they will be open to what you have to say. This will not only improve their skill set, but yours as well. Knowing that you can see things others may not, and having that vision accepted, is quite the self-confidence builder.

There is a lot of truth in the old adage "It's not what you say, but how you say it." If someone thinks that you are going to just blast her, her ability to take in your wisdom, no matter how great, will be diminished. Never judge or reject a person's ideas or desires without first considering them. If you have a difference of opinion, that's fine, as long as you express it with kindness.

Also, speak in a pleasant tone, and remember to smile. Almost half of communication is tonal, and a little more than half is visual. Speaking in a sincere and calming tone will let the other party know you are coming from a caring place. This is how self-confident people communicate.

57. Giving a Boost

You give but little when you give of your possessions. It is when you give of yourself that you truly give.
—Kahlil Gibran, *The Prophet*

Your ability to give a loved one, friend, or coworker an emotional boost when he is feeling badly is a better cure than Prozac. When life is kicking sand in your face, it's natural to turn to someone who you know cares and respects you. If that person can really be there for you with emotional support and kind words of encouragement, it can make a big difference in how you feel. It's almost too simple.

If you have difficulty giving that kind of support or accepting it, you need to look at your state of mind and make a few adjustments. Perhaps you are projecting your feelings of distrust in the world, or your angst about those unjust criticisms from your boss, but that isn't going to help you. What will help is giving and receiving positive input from those closest to you.

We all push others away from time to time—it's human, but it's also destructive and will erode any confidence you may have left after a tough day. Do an honest evaluation of your ability (or inability) to take in the positive, and also on how you expel your negative emotions. Even if you only slightly use emotions as a weapon, that's a great way to start a war, so check yourself out.

The calm that exudes through your mind and body when someone is there to make it all better will ease your pain. And when you feel better, you can think more clearly about how best to deal with the situation. Once you have a good game plan, not only will your discomfort improve, but your confidence about dealing with the situation will increase as well.

Look, the world isn't fair, and there are always going to be times when we all need a cheerleader (pom-poms are optional). Being there for someone in need is a gift you are giving to the person who isn't feeling at the top of her game, and it is returned in a number of ways. The most obvious is that the mood in the air will be lighter, and this affects both of you.

Saying something like, "I know you're worried, but we'll get through this together [or as a team]," or

"You've always landed on your feet, so why should this time be any different?" will give her a much-needed boost. Just being there while she sits and sulks a little is also fine. Remember that we all need to process our grief, no matter where it comes from.

Things in your life have mostly worked out. Reminding yourself and those around you of this, and looking at what you've been through while taking stock of where you are now, is also a very helpful tool.

Getting and giving an emotional boost to or from someone who is on your team may be what this whole world is all about. And it sure feels great.

58. You Can Juggle

I'd rather be in Philadelphia.
—The epitaph of W.C. Fields, who once said about the City of Brotherly Love, "Ahh, yes, Philadelphia; I spent two weeks there one night."

Old-time comedian W.C. Fields was actually one of the best jugglers in the world—maybe *the* best in his day—and the confidence that talent gave him had to have helped propel him to stardom. You almost never saw him juggle in a movie, but he wrote, directed, produced, acted, did his own stunts, and promoted and made a career out of being himself. I think that qualifies as juggling, and it is a testament to trusting his inner strength.

Though his feet of clay were legendary, along with his drinking and dislike of children, his imperfections couldn't shake his belief in himself. And millions, to this day, remember and love his work. He built something from what most would see as nothing: being a great juggler.

Learning how to juggle may seem like a waste of time, but I have taught hundreds of people, from CEOs to alcoholics in rehab, how to juggle. Learning this little skill can help anyone lift himself out of his self-made pit and put a smile on his face. You see, along with the hand-eye coordination and the increased ability to focus, juggling is also fun, and we all would like to be able to do it. The good news here is that we all *can* do it, and it really doesn't take much time or talent.

Obviously, I can't show you how to juggle in my book, but there's a great little book that comes with some juggling cubes (which don't roll away as easily as balls) by Klutz, and a few DVDs also available.

If this chapter is ruffling your feathers and you think it's a waste of time, I urge you to remember that a researcher who has personally experienced the positive effects of this process is the one who is writing it. And you probably haven't had a good belly laugh in way too long, which is not allowing you to be your most creative and inventive self. Look it up and you'll see the research backs my claim.

Sometimes putting aside your attitude and allowing yourself to be in a receptive mode will make the difference between a good life experience and a bad one.

Using your strength to put aside whatever is working you at the moment and developing a new skill is worth your valuable time because it's not *what* you learn that's important; it's the pride you get from learning it. The added benefit is that you now know you don't have to be the victim of those old negative emotions that came with past struggles.

My business partner and I break out the juggling balls every now and then when we're brainstorming. After you get the basics down you can do tricks, and you may find that this seemingly mindless activity actually stimulates your thinking and creativity.

I know it sounds a little silly, but I don't know one person who can juggle who'd give it back, because, on some level, learning how and getting better at it made them feel better about themselves.

59. Inner Strength

We confide in our strength, without boasting of it;
we respect that of others, without fearing it.
—Thomas Jefferson

The power within you is what you call upon when the chips are down and you consider cashing in. Using your most creative inner resources to pull yourself up by your bootstraps will give you the sense that you can deal with anything life throws at you.

We all have strength in various areas; wouldn't it be great if we could transfer it around? Imagine putting all your brainpower into your muscles when you have to lift a couch, or channeling your emotional fortitude into your problem-solving skill set. You'd be invincible, and that is exactly what those who achieve greatness are. The only difference between them and you is that they know how to access and direct their strengths. The good news here is that this is a skill set you can learn.

One of the first things the greats have learned about summoning their inner strength when needed is that they have to believe they can do it. That usually means they've practiced, rehearsed, and polished their skill set well enough to know they can always come up with an answer or plan their way out of a jam.

People who seemingly successfully fly by the seat of their pants have usually put a lot of time into their abilities. It only looks easy because that is part of the process. Your strength doesn't want to (or need to) get diluted by unnecessary struggle. So making it look easy is really an attitudinal adjustment with a purpose. Don't waste your energy; do what you can the best way you know how, and trust that the results will be successful.

Inner strength is pure and comes without bravado, because bravado is a waste of time. Inner strength is a quiet victory that doesn't require ticker-tape parades or even outside acknowledgment (thought that seldom hurts). When you know that something requires your best work, succeeding at it is usually enough of a reward.

Summoning up your inner strength is a bit of an art form. Some people need to first quiet themselves to find their reservoir, and others need to prime themselves with communication, visualization, or even exercise.

Another great tool for reaching into your personal bag of tricks is hindsight. Telling yourself you have survived worse and you will survive whatever challenge is facing you at the moment will give you additional reserves from which to pull. Knowing that you have succeeded with much bigger issues is a great confidence-booster, even if the new dilemma is totally unexpected or unusual.

Your inner strength is a tool that is always with you. Think of it as the Swiss Army Knife of your psyche: You have all the tools you need right in your pocket. All you have to do is to reach in and pull them out. I know that sometimes, when we are stressed, we can easily forget to use our internal resources, and, of course, that is the time when we need them most.

So the next time you are stressed out or in over your head, think about how you've dealt with other difficult moments and trust that you have it within yourself to deal with this one as well. The real truth is that you have all the inner strength you need.

60. Enlightenment: It's Not Just for Gurus Anymore

The journey of a thousand miles begins with a single step.
—Lao Tzu

When we think about enlightened people, very few come to mind: Spiritual masters such as Jesus, Buddha, and Moses; business icons like Warren Buffett, Lee Iacocca, and Bill Gates; artists like Elvis, The Beatles, and Ozzie Osborne (okay, maybe not him) have all enlightened us and helped us define our lives. The ability to feel enlightened keeps us solid in our choices and decisions.

We take in what the enlightened have to say because they have proven themselves with time. The spiritual masters took decades to become who they were, and we have had centuries to accept their teachings. The masters of the arts and business have had substantially less time to be absorbed into our psyches, but their reputations are growing. Think about it: Why else would Warren Buffett's nickname be "The Oracle of Omaha?"

These people have earned their enlightenment, and you have the same ability. The good news is that you don't have to be a master (or dead) to acquire it, and the even better news is that there are many different types of enlightenment. So there is no need to compare yourself to a religious leader or a burnt-out rocker.

The enlightened leader knows how to boost confidence when business is slow. The enlightened teacher knows when his or her students need to feel better about themselves in order to succeed. The enlightened friend knows when someone needs a shoulder to cry on, and that words need not be spoken, because it just feels safer when someone is there to share our troubles. We all have different enlightenments, and that is as it should be. No one can be enlightened in all areas, so there is no reason for you to beat yourself up because you missed a step or two. I mean, really, would an enlightened person even think along those lines?

Here's the real deal on enlightenment: It is a lifelong process that can only make you feel more confident about yourself as you stumble through its attainment. Your thoughts may change with the wind, but your enlightened spirit is unshakable.

I always thought the word GURU meant "Gee-You-Are-You."

61. Learn to Love Yourself

Believe in yourself! Have faith in your abilities! Without a humble but reasonable confidence in your own powers you cannot be successful or happy.
—Norman Vincent Peale

Self-love may be one of the most underutilized sources of our esteem. We can be harder on ourselves than on any other person. Consciously giving yourself a break, and not falling into the trap of self-denigration, will allow you to save your energy for the important parts of life and help you keep your confidence intact.

Look, there is a big difference between self-love and narcissism. People who are narcissistic don't love themselves; they are *in* love *with* themselves, so there isn't any room in their hearts for anyone or anything else. But those who have worked and learned to love themselves not only have the ability to take in positive energy from other people, but they can also give it back tenfold.

Our confidence can't flourish when we don't love ourselves because there will always be a reason we don't feel deserving of any love—not from within, from another person, or even from God. People who beat themselves up in this way have very difficult lives and relationships. Even thought this is a very difficult situation, there are a number of ways you can begin to develop self-love and ensure your confidence.

If you are negatively judgmental toward your own way of being, no one is going to be able to give you a course correction that you will hear. This one has to come from inside your own head and heart. Making the realization that you don't like your life, and then digging deeper and discovering that what you don't like is who you have become, is a life-altering process. The good news here is that the person you really are and the one you have become may be vastly different people. You have to get in touch with your core values and make sure you are living them. If not, it will cause a disconnect within the part of your brain that governs self-esteem, and you won't be able to rationalize how you feel internally.

Stopping behaviors that cause you to dislike or make you unable to love yourself is like changing a tire.

First you have to stop and assess the damage. Which tire is it? Is it really flat or just low? Once you have discovered and admitted that there is a problem, you need to make sure you have the strength and the tools to fix it. So you look in the trunk and make sure your spare tire is good and that you have a jack and a lug wrench. For repairing a flat emotional psyche, first look at your spare: Can you change your behaviors enough to make a significant impact on your life and self-love? Also make sure you have the tools you need, such as a good and honest support structure, some basic knowledge about personal growth, and perhaps a good therapist to help you navigate the rough roads ahead. If not, it is imperative that you create some kind of personal growth strategy and support. Without it, getting to your destination will be much more difficult, if not impossible.

With the basic tools, you will not only be able to learn to love yourself, but you will also find that those around you will like you more, and that can only add to your self-esteem.

62. Appreciate Who You Are

The only thing that stands between a man and what he wants from life is often merely the will to try it and the faith to believe that it is possible.
—Richard M. Devos

Being fulfilled as a person can't help but make you feel more self-confident. Fulfillment isn't about having it all; it is about appreciating what you do have.

Even if you haven't reached your goals yet, you can and should be fulfilled in the process of getting there. If not, it could be because you are heading in the wrong direction and your psyche is telling you that something isn't feeling quite right. We have to learn to listen to (and perhaps translate) these messages that come from our unconscious, as they offer a ton of information of which we probably haven't become fully aware.

In addition, one's sense of fulfillment changes as we mature. As children we feel quite good when we are fed, changed, and nurtured. As teens we want popularity and a sense that we are cool enough. When we finally enter adulthood, the direction our fulfillment takes usually changes because we start to consider the pros and cons of marriage, children, working for a company, or starting our own business—all of which we hope will lead us to the Holy Grail of personal fulfillment. The problem is that our needs and desires often change with time, and this is why it is so important to be confident about the choices you make when you build your life, no matter what your age.

Look, if you know you are not a "kid person," raising a family, though totally fulfilling for millions of people, may not work for you. Even though your parents did it and everyone else may be doing it, you must make sure that it is the right decision for you.

Making big life decisions because someone you are with or related to wants it for you isn't going to make you happy. It's understandable that you don't want to disappoint your loved ones, but the real truth is that, if you're not confident that you are making the right decision, talk about it, write about it, and think about it long and hard before moving forward. Be unshakable in your confidence because these life choices will likely be with you forever.

It is also important to understand that fulfillment responds to confidence much in the same way that doing good creates self-respect. When you are feeling good about what you are doing, and believe it is the right thing to do, it can't help but make you feel better about your life and those in it.

Looking for fulfillment could also mean really looking at what you already have. Dorothy had to take a trip to Oz to realize that everything she ever wanted was right there in her own backyard. She finally understood, after witches, lions, tigers, and bears, as well as flying monkeys, that fulfillment isn't about getting what you want; it's about appreciating what you already have. And Toto, too.

63. Got Energy?

*Part of being a champ is acting like a champ.
You have to learn how to win and not run away
when you lose. Everyone has bad stretches and real
successes. Either way, you have to be careful not
to lose your confidence or get too confident.*
—Nancy Kerrigan

Emotional energy feeds our minds and hearts and gives us the physical ability to move our lives forward. When you don't have energy you can't feel good about yourself or anything else, and the best way to get it is to put more of it out. I know this sounds a little counter-intuitive, but sometimes we all need to give ourselves a helping hand when we're feeling low and there's nobody else around to help us get out of our own way.

These can be times that try our souls—or feed them, depending on how we approach what's in front of us. If you give in to your lows you will continue to sink lower. But if you just put out a little energy, by doing almost anything, you will at the very least not get any worse. It is also quite likely that you will not only feel better in the moment, but you will also have begun to create the knowledge that you can pull yourself out of the blues, and that is very empowering.

The next step is to make replacing a low moment with some positive energy a regular habit. Whenever low moments hit me, I go outside and sit by the lake. I'm usually feeling human again after about 10 minutes.

Others might go for a run or read a book; whatever works for you is the right thing.

On the other hand, if you are truly physically exhausted, maybe the best thing for you to do is to go to bed and get some rest, even if it's the middle of the day. I know many high-powered executives who take "power naps" for 20 to 50 minutes (any longer and you begin another sleep cycle), which perks them up for the rest of the day. Every 5 year old on the planet knows that napping can be a great energy-booster—maybe we should take a lesson.

The late-afternoon lows are so human that a few centuries ago the British created "tea time." That little caffeine boost gives many people the energy they need to make it through the rest of the day. There are also those ubiquitous energy drinks, and if they work for you that may be an answer, but don't overdo it.

Once you find ways to give yourself an energy boost, your confidence level rises right along with your energy.

64. Selflessness Raises Your Self-Worth

Real love is when you become selfless and you are more concerned about your mate's or children's egos than your own. You're now a giver instead of a taker.
—Sylvester Stallone

That quality of putting others before yourself is a great way to build your self-esteem and contribute to those who need you at the same time. If you do nothing else today, help someone who needs it and then just see how you feel.

Webster defines selflessness as "having no concern for one's self," and I have to disagree with my old friend Merriam. It's not about a lack of concern for one's self. It's the "put your own oxygen mask on first" idea: If you are selfless to the point of self-destruction, you're not really helping anyone, and you're missing the point.

Being selfless raises your sense of self-worth, and that makes you better at whatever it is you're giving to others. Really knowing you're on the right path and giving of your heart can't help but make you feel better about yourself.

Although sometimes the people to whom we give are ungrateful, for the most part they are appreciative. That being said, I think that giving anonymously is great for boosting your confidence. You know you're doing the right thing, but you don't need a payoff, and that is the essence of a self-actualized human being. All I can say is thank you for doing what you do.

65. Trusting Yourself

Trust yourself. You know more than you think you do.
—Benjamin Spock, MD

Trust must first be given to yourself, because not having it works directly against your self-confidence. Believe that you are here for the right reasons and your full participation in life is valuable to those around you.

If this is not something you can do in your own mind, then start asking people you know and who care for you if you have made a difference in their lives. When we can't see our worth in the world it is hard to trust that we deserve to be here, or for good things to happen around us. Getting validation from those close to you will help you see that you have contributed to the lives of people who are important to you, and perhaps also to the world at large.

Think of the things in your life you are proud of. There are a number of them, but you may have to spend a little time remembering that you loved restoring that old antique dresser and did a great job, or that time you really saved someone (or yourself) a ton of money with a simple suggestion. You have good instincts and are deserving of trust, but you have to find it within yourself in order to take your self-confidence up a notch.

66. Effectively Express Emotions

To give vent now and then to his feelings, whether of pleasure or discontent, is a great ease to a man's heart.
—Francesco Guicciardini

Being in touch with your feelings will make you a better person, as well as a better parent and partner. Being true to your emotions can't help but make you feel better about yourself because you're able to be authentic.

When we choose to bury our feelings we act differently. We may not make ourselves available to others, and withdraw from people, or we're just not fully engaged when we are available. At other times, we can react inappropriately because our emotions are pulling us in a different direction than we really want or need to go in. When you express how you really feel (in an appropriate manner), problems get solved, relationship issues get resolved, and life gets easier. In addition, you will like your life (and yourself) better because you're not holding on to unhealed or confusing feelings.

Expressing what you really feel is very freeing as well as empowering. Sometimes you have to hold back speaking your truth because the situation requires that you do so. For example, if there are other people (especially children) in the room, or you're coming from a place of anger, double-check to make sure you're speaking in a tone that won't offend or upset. The purpose of expressing your emotions is to convey your true feelings and to be an open and honest person, not to embarrass or blast another human being.

Sometimes we need to express our pain and sadness, and many people are afraid to do so because they fear that, once they get started, they may not be able to stop. This is a common misconception, as depressing thoughts distort your thinking and you don't perceive the world correctly during those times. The real truth is that by letting the tears flow, you are letting out what hurts while making more room in your heart for positive thoughts and feelings. Expressing your pain is actually a good way to make it stop.

Most of us are far better at talking about what we don't like than what we enjoy or what touches us deeply. Take the time to tell someone who has made your life a little better that she has done so, and you will also feel better for having said it. Do your best to spend as much energy expressing your positive feelings as you do the negative ones. Once you create an emotional balance, your life starts to make more sense.

Ultimately, we all want to experience and share the good stuff more than the toxic energies that protrude throughout our days, but it can take a little while to develop the habit. It's not as much about practicing as it is about how you come across and what that really feels like when you say what's truly going on inside your head.

When you open your mouth, you are also opening your heart, and knowing that someone truly hears what you are feeling and "gets" you is not just a confidence boost; it's soothing to your soul.

67. The Butterfly Effect

The fluttering of a butterfly's wings can effect
climate changes on the other side of the planet.
—Paul Erlich

The ability to influence the world in a positive way is incredibly empowering. Leaving the planet a tiny bit better than you found it will bring meaning to anyone's life.

Unfortunately the opposite is also true: If you have no effect on those around you, it makes you feel impotent. There is a false sense of power to be gained by having a negative effect, but those behaviors are reserved for children, or adults who are not emotionally stable. If you want to feel good about yourself, work to have a positive effect in all that you do.

A theory called "The Butterfly Effect" proposes that if we were able to go back in time to prehistoric days and accidentally killed a mere butterfly, the evolution of the entire planet could change. The first use of the term also suggested that the mere flapping of a butterfly's wings could change weather patterns on the other side of the globe, causing or preventing hurricanes and other natural disasters.

Applying this theory to your own life, if you release something beautiful or loving into your surroundings, you are having a life-enhancing effect on the world. Even a seemingly insignificant act, such as letting someone into traffic ahead of you, can have far-reaching and life-altering repercussions: If the person you let in front of you was prone to driving too fast so that he could get to his kid's soccer game on time, maybe you prevented him from getting into an accident. Knowing that even your most benign actions can have positive effects on the world can't help but boost your sense of self-worth.

68. Motivation: Find It and Keep It

First thing every morning before you arise say out loud, I believe.
—Norman Vincent Peale

Motivation is what propels us to the next level of life. Without the strong desire to move forward, most people just sit and wait for life to happen to them. Such people usually get less out of their lives, are unable to contribute to the well-being of humanity, and are generally dissatisfied with themselves.

Just hearing the word *motivation* conjures up visions of corporate leaders trying to pump up their staff or cheerleaders inspiring the home team to "block that kick," but the most powerful form of motivation is the type that comes from within us. When we have that drive, and the self-assurance that we can hit the mark, we are almost unstoppable.

For some the vision of the goal is all that's needed. Others need a deeper reason to become motivated, and once that is found, it sends signals to your brain that you are ready, willing, and able to take the next challenge head-on. It lets us feel our own personal power, and that's a very potent force.

Wanting to have a positive impact on those around you, or the world at large, is a great way to motivate yourself; it is also very life-enhancing. For many, that goal is what gets them out of bed in the morning and puts a smile on their face throughout the day.

For those who have trouble finding motivation, perhaps looking at it in a different light will be helpful. For example, if you heard all your life that you lacked motivation, you may be rebelling against the people who told you that and allowing it to become a self-fulfilling prophesy by not doing anything to change it. The truth here is that you are feeling hurt by someone who didn't believe in you, and if you give that person free rent in your head it's going to be very hard to disengage the thoughts.

Try blocking out or erasing those old tapes, which may take a few tries. For some, filling their mind with thoughts or affirmations such as "I can do it" or "I'm good at this" will help. Letting go of unwanted thoughts will assist you in finding the motivation that almost always lies beneath them. Look, if you didn't want to feel better about yourself, you wouldn't be reading this, so you *are* motivated, but you may be a little scared to get in touch with it and try because you are afraid of failing.

The truth is that, if you want something, and you can't summon the energy to get motivated about getting it, then you really don't want it. Whether it's self-confidence or a yacht, you have to be motivated to gather your forces together and start moving toward your goal. What anyone else thinks or does shouldn't stop you. Support is great, but success in life requires you to sometimes be self-motivated in order to get where you want to go. Remember that happiness comes from moving toward what you want, not from getting it.

69. An Attitude of Gratitude

As we express our gratitude, we must never forget that the highest appreciation is not to utter words, but to live by them.
—John Fitzgerald Kennedy

Some years are better than others. The past few have been more difficult largely due to the economic crisis that has put millions out of work and millions more in fear of being next. Add to that the lost savings, lost homes, and children moving back in to their parents' homes (perhaps with their own kids), and many are having difficulty finding things for which to be grateful and feel confident about in the years ahead.

Well, if you're one who has recently moved or taken in family, you may have a more crowded house, but you also have more love. Some people are fortunate enough to have family members they truly enjoy being around, and so having them live with you is more of a benefit than an inconvenience. Even if you don't really care for the situation, the truth is that it won't last forever, and, as those of us who have been in the same position know, in the end it will leave you with some treasured memories. There is also the side benefit that you have an extra pair of hands when you're bringing in the groceries, and an extra boost when you need some external confidence-building.

For those who are out of work or earning less (and that would be most of us), I'm hearing that, after an adjustment period of getting used to living with less, life is pretty much the same. There are challenges, like budgeting or taking on another job, and people are perhaps a bit wearier at the end of the day, but also feeling grateful that they can once again provide for their families.

I know a large number of people who are re-educating themselves. Going back to college or trade school in mid-life may not be all that attractive to some, but I did it a couple of recessions ago and I will be forever grateful I made the choice. The thought is daunting, and the workload scary, but the results are greater self-esteem, a stable income, and the joy of doing something you love. Returning to school is not a sign of failure; by doing so you are showing the world (and yourself) that you have the mettle to withstand what is thrown at you, and the creativity to figure a way out. You are more than a survivor; you are a thriver—something else to help you boost your confidence level.

If life is holding you down in any area, this attitude can help you take stock of what you have and what potential you have yet to uncover. We all know that adversity makes us stronger, but for those who have been battling the forces of the economy, it can be a little hard to see past the losses and envision a brighter future. Maybe it won't happen next year, but sooner or later things will get better, and when they do, I think you will see that your priorities have also shifted; the most important thing in life will always be the love we have around us. Be truly grateful for it, as it gives you a type of confidence that nothing else can.

70. Emotional Fitness in the Workplace

Confidence is contagious, and so is lack of confidence, and a customer will recognize both.
—Vincent Lombardi

Confidence training is a necessity in the workplace, and it must include helping people understand their emotions. Contrary to popular myth, emotional people are passionate people, and passionate people make things happen. They create change and shake things up. Their passion begets persistence, and they give the companies they work for a healthy dose of energy and productivity.

Of course, in the minds of many business owners and senior managers, emotions are bad; managers want everything to be detached, cool, and objective. But at the same time they want employees to be motivated and passionate, and they spend countless hours and huge amounts of money trying to get them pumped up about their jobs. But passion itself is a form of emotion—a healthy form—so it would be self-defeating to ban emotions from the workplace, even if you could. What works best is to help people feel confident about their emotions so they are expressed in a cogent manner rather than a rant.

The challenge for businesses is to foster confidence while keeping a lack of it from destroying the company. There's no question that negative emotions can cause employees to perform erratically, engage in blaming and name-calling, and ultimately sabotage the goals of management. If negative and unhealed emotions are not addressed, a company can lose good employees and even good customers and clients. The company can go into a downward spiral from which it may never recover. Whether they like it or not, today's executives spend half their time being therapists to their staff, and it's crucial that they be *good* therapists and help team members feel confident about themselves and their company.

71. You Look Marvelous

The difference between a man of sense and a fop is that the fop values himself upon his dress, and the man of sense laughs at it, at the same time he knows he must not neglect it.
—Lord Chesterfield

Long before "Dress for Success" hit the market, people were not just judged by their appearance: Their lives were dictated by it. In olden times, paupers and nobles could be told apart from a distance by their clothes (and maybe the way they smelled). Clothing has always been a way of showing what you want others to see.

Many people dress to impress because they want others to perceive them in a specific way. Corporate executives wear power suits and ties, and rock stars (and wannabes) use piercings, leather, and tattoos to create an image for their fans. People in all walks of life dress not just for success but also for effect—both good and bad.

Your appearance can also dictate how you feel about yourself. If you think you're sexy sitting around in two-year-old sweats, your self-image may need a slight tune-up. When you get dressed in the morning (or, if you're a rock star, in the afternoon) the clothes you choose will make you feel a certain way. If you like that feeling, you will be empowered; if you don't, your confidence level will be shaken to one degree or another.

A friend of mine coined the phrase *manicured depression*. Whenever she was feeling a little down she went and got a manicure and/or pedicure, put on something that made her feel good about herself, and strutted through the mall. Getting looks of approval from strangers made her feel better, and then she would deal with whatever problem was vexing her at the moment from a place of self-assurance.

If you're not feeling all that good about yourself, try her technique (okay guys, you can pass on the "mani-pedi"; have your shoes shined instead). Giving ourselves the gift of looking good makes most of us feel better about life. It also helps others see us at our best, and, though we may not actually be feeling that way at the moment, looking and feeling great can lead us to it.

So break out the formal gown or the tux and do yourself up to the nines, stand in front of the mirror, and just let yourself feel good about the person you see. The truth is, you deserve it.

72. Forgive Your Way to Confidence

The weak can never forgive. Forgiveness is the attribute of the strong.
—Mahatma Gandhi

If you hold on to toxic feelings of resentment and can't seem to let go of a grudge, you are actually holding yourself back from having a better life. Learning how to forgive those who have wronged you and also forgive yourself is one of the tools necessary to keep your confidence level solid.

Forgiveness is not a magical spell that will immediately turn your world around and make everything okay, but the principle is sound. The amounts of negative energy you have to hold on to in order to stay upset can cause you pain and certainly hold you back. It can also do damage to your physical and your emotional well-being.

Before you can forgive another, it may be necessary to forgive yourself. If you aren't sure why or even if you are angry with yourself, you need to get in touch with the resentful feeling and its cause. Just sit quietly and ask yourself what you have done or avoided that makes you feel insecure. Perhaps you just need to say you are sorry to yourself or someone else. It may take some additional introspection to truly let this negative feeling go, but the process will give you incredible relief.

You will not be able to move forward in your life if you allow anger at yourself or someone else to run through your psyche. When that happens, your brain continually tells you that you're not good enough, and eventually you start to believe it, and your behaviors will follow that very inappropriate lead.

True remorse is a part of the process, whether it be forgiving yourself or another, or feeling sorry for the wrongs that were committed. Being available to make amends is a necessity if you want to let go of the pain.

The idea of atonement encapsulates how forgiveness works. Making the realization of any misdeeds, appropriately apologizing, and asking for (or offering) forgiveness will allow you to let go of the pain and move forward with the rest of your life.

Knowing that you can forgive yourself and those who have wronged you can't help but make you a more self-assured human being.

73. Learn to Love Mondays

If you have a job without any aggravations, you don't have a job.
—Malcolm S. Forbes

More heart attacks, strokes, suicides, sicknesses, and accidents occur on Monday mornings than any other day of the week. Research suggests that this is because people are distracted and unhappy when the weekend is over and they have to go to jobs they don't resonate with. If the beginning of your week makes you want to change the calendar or your career, you may want to spend a few moments taking a good look at why.

We have all had the Monday blahs sometimes. It's pretty human to want to avoid the commute, the grind, or a boss who seems to enjoy giving you a hard time. There is also the pressure of having to show your worth in a world where jobs are becoming more difficult to find and keep. Even the best and the brightest have off days and times when they wish they were doing something different. It's only human.

Now more than ever, hanging in there is important, and finding ways to make it more comfortable is clearly a necessity.

It can help to reassess how you look at your work and reduce any pressure that you may be adding on your own. If you know that your position is secure, but can't summon up the energy to enjoy that fact, start thinking about what the 10-plus percent of people who don't have a gig at the moment might be doing (and fearing) in their lives. If that doesn't make you grateful for what you have, despite the fact that you feel a little overworked or underappreciated, then you need to take a hard look at what else might be taking away your motivation.

If you don't feel secure about your job, and you believe that things are going to get worse, it becomes even more difficult to face the week ahead. The old saying that "When the going gets tough, the tough get going" is very appropriate here. This is definitely not the time to rest on your laurels and wait for something better to come along.

I suggest making the best impression you can on a daily basis. You can turn getting a different job or starting a home-based business into your new hobby.

You can also get the whole family involved in a little weekend business like a garage sale. Right now, if you aren't putting in some extra time and days, you need to think about doing so.

The upside is that by doing it as a family you have more time for your loved ones. And everyone will appreciate your willingness to take care of business during a time now being referred to as the Great Recession.

Learning to look forward to Mondays may not be something you're wired for, but if you can make it happen, your world is going to feel a lot better. Accepting that work is a part of life, and doing whatever you can to keep your dreams alive while shining at your day job, is the only way you can make your dreams a reality.

74. Never Accept Unacceptable Behavior

Love all, trust a few, do wrong to none.
—William Shakespeare

Confident people do not need to accept unacceptable behavior from another person. When someone behaves inappropriately or is potentially abusive, your best option is to let her know what you see, and stop the bad behavior in its tracks.

By doing so you are setting a boundary for yourself that will serve you well. If you don't, when people see that you are willing to let them do or say things that are questionable, you are actually giving them permission to continue doing so.

Saying "stop" or, if necessary, leaving the room (or asking the other person to) lets him know he has crossed a line and signals him not to do it again. Discussing the offending behaviors may be necessary, and important if you want to save the relationship, so don't just point to the door; let people know you are willing to talk about it.

Do not let yourself be abused. It will erode your confidence faster than anything else I can think of.

75. Plan B

We all have big changes in our lives that are more or less a second chance.
—Harrison Ford

Because many things don't go as well as we would like them to, it's a great idea to have a "Plan B." Having fallback plans can't help but make you feel better about the outcome of any situation, and it is a common denominator among very self-confident people.

Anyone who has had more than one failure in her life can tell you that having another path to take probably saved her bacon a time or two. I'm a big one for contingency plans. If you are an entrepreneur, in the arts or media, or you have all your eggs in one basket, a Plan B is essential.

Knowing that if you lose the farm you have a condo you can go to makes you feel safer in the world. I know a number of people who have motor homes, and one of the reasons they do is, as they jokingly say, it's their "in case" home. During the last big earthquake here in Los Angeles, many people who had them were very grateful—and those of us who didn't were envious.

With the world economy in turmoil, creating some kind of additional income stream is also a good idea. The jeweler who is also a great designer or builder, the computer geek who can also teach school, or the PR person who is a closet novelist can all find a way to thrive even if their current position disappears.

Backup plans don't have to be new ideas—I continue to use aspects of everything I've ever done. My days on stage playing guitar have made me a better public speaker, which makes me a good radio host. The energy I put into songs and poems has helped them become columns and books. The years I spent running my own business give me the insight to help others streamline theirs. And all of my experiences have made me a confident and successful therapist. Every talent and ability you have can be built upon and also used again. Not that I'd ever again want to be on a tour bus with six smelly guys for eight weeks, but if I had to I could still put food on the table by humming and strumming.

There's another potential upside here: Sometimes your original plan and your backup can work at the same time. I still counsel, consult, write, and speak to groups all over the world. In years when the speaking business got very slow (such as after 9/11 and then the financial crisis), I spent more time writing and counseling. When there was a lull between books, I put more energy into my radio show and business consulting, and did pro-bono events. Having multiple options gives you the sense that, if any one thing went away, you'd have other gigs that would more than fill the gap.

So get a little creative. Look at your past accomplishments and your current talents. A Plan B is only an idea away.

By the way, this Plan B thing works in life, but not in relationships. Having a backup mate is only going to erode your current relationship and cause heartache for everyone involved. Enough said.

76. Practice, Practice, Practice

The more you sweat in practice, the less you bleed in battle.
—Anonymous

The good news is that even if you don't have confidence, you can learn to find it. There's an old joke about a tourist asking someone on the streets of New York how to get to Carnegie Hall. The stranger responded, "Practice, young man, practice." Start practicing and polishing your act, whatever it may be.

When you know you're great at what you do, your confidence is far less likely to be shaken.

Practice, even if you're doing the same thing over and over, doesn't have to be boring. Yes, musicians play scales for hours and athletes run endless drills, but at the same time they are also mentally on stage or at a meet visualizing their success. Using practice in this manner not only keeps them in shape to do what they do, but it also helps them to get better.

As a writer, I believe (and some will disagree) that there are very few practice exercises to do other than writing, but some people like to read to warm up, and others use outlines or notes to help them get started. All of these preparations are good practice for creating a piece or a performance you will feel good about.

A famous musician once said that if he didn't practice for one day he would notice a difference. If he didn't practice for two days his teacher would notice, and if he didn't practice for three days the audience would notice. And so he sits at the keyboard every day and keeps his art honed and his confidence high.

The trick is to make practicing something you enjoy doing every day. Sometimes you have to do a little mental gymnastics to make that thought a reality. If you only like practicing because it makes you better at what you do, that's fine because that little piece of positive attitude will help you get to the next level and continue to refine your skill set. But it will make your practice sessions much easier if you feel some joy in the process. We all know the truth that practice makes perfect. What some fail to realize is that practice also boosts your self-confidence.

77. Don't Be Owned by What You Desire

Every day I get up and look through the Forbes list of the richest people in America. If I'm not there, I go to work.
—Robert Orb

Desire is one of our most powerful motivating forces, but it is wise to be sure that what you want will improve your life and the lives of those you care for. Whether it's a person, place, position, or object, wanting something too much can make you do things that go against your value system, and that may be far more painful than not getting what you want.

To covet someone who is attached or unavailable will only bring pain to you and perhaps to another. If you are in a relationship and you are feeling desire for a person other than your partner, the one who shares your bed will feel it on some level. If this has ever happened to you, remember how you felt when your mate emotionally pulled away. You may not be sure of what you are feeling, but you know that something isn't quite right. And then the relationship is thrown off balance.

At this point you start to look at what you might not like about the person you are with and how much better the one you desire will fit into your life. Most of this happens in your own head. Keep in mind that regardless of how many "moments" you've experienced with the object of your desire, you really don't know what life would be like with him.

If what you want is beyond your financial means, going into debt (especially in this economy) is at the very least unwise, and could, at worst, ruin your chances of achieving the American Dream. Spending money you don't have on something you don't actually need is like trying to fill a bottomless pit in your soul.

The emptiness in your heart can never be filled this way. If you're living beyond your means, take a good, strong look at your behavior. It may be smart to cut up some credit cards or block the home shopping channels on your television. Simple acts such as these won't automatically stop you from spending what you don't have, but it will remind you that you need to change this part of your life.

Most people want to move forward or up in their lives. We think of this as ambition, and it's usually a very good thing, unless it goes blind. Achievement at any cost can be emotionally expensive and actually cripple your upward mobility, and you will also alienate the people who would have supported you.

The best way to build your career is to create a support team that works together to achieve the kind of success and recognition to which you aspire. It takes more time, but it will make you better, and your position will last a lot longer than if you got it by stepping over your coworkers.

Desire, when used appropriately, will help you get what you want. Just make sure that keeping your integrity is part of the goal.

78. Class Up Your Act

Class is an aura of confidence that is being sure
without being cocky. Class has nothing to do with
money. Class never runs scared. It is self-discipline
and self-knowledge. It's the sure-footedness that
comes with having proved you can meet life.
— Ann Landers

I met actor Martin Sheen at a rally to support a local organization that helps the homeless. When I was introduced to him, he stuck out his hand to shake mine and said, "Hi, I'm Martin Sheen." Two thoughts went through my mind: the first, "Duh!", and the second, how classy it was of him not to assume that I knew him just because he was the star of the number-one television show at the time (*The West Wing*).

There are two kinds of people in the world: those who have class and those who don't. The ones who do are unassuming, gracious, and kind. They radiate an aura of confidence and warmth. The others are the quintessential jerks we have all met or heard about. Your mission—should you decide to accept it—is to be a class act. If self-confidence gives you anything at all, for the sake of the people who care for you, let it be that.

79. Second Thoughts

*If you don't get everything you want, think of the
things you don't get that you don't want.*

—Oscar Wilde

Whoever said it wasn't okay to change your mind?
Most people, even very confident people, make choices
they believe are wise and then have second thoughts.
It's not neurotic; it's normal. Rethinking a decision—
be it on a small purchase or in a large business deal—
can make you doubt yourself, so it's wise to understand
that process so you can deal with it as well as possible.

In terms of a financial choice, some call it *buyer's
remorse*. We've all made a substantial purchase and
then wondered if we've done the right thing—we have
thoughts about the cost versus what we are getting,
looking at our income and the economy, and then there's
the "did I get the best deal I could" machinations that
go through our now totally confused mind. Buying a
new home, refinancing, or purchasing a big-ticket item
such as a car or a vacation can make you beat yourself
up to the point that, no matter how great the holiday
or the item, you can't enjoy yourself (or the new car,
house, or flat-screen TV).

None of us can make all the right decisions. If you are
used to almost always being correct in your choices, then
making mistakes or having second thoughts becomes
even more uncomfortable. But second-guessing is also
an opportunity to tune in to your confidence level and

ask yourself how deeply your decision will affect you in the big picture. In most cases, even with the largest purchases or decisions, there is a way to change course.

If you don't feel good about yourself because of a decision, other than in the case of plastic surgery, you can usually reverse it. Most things you buy can be returned, although sometimes you have to pay a "restocking" charge or a "buy-down" fee. Renegotiations in these cases are important because you can't accept a deal that's going to make you feel like a doormat.

The post-decision fear is that, even if you don't lose any money, you could lose face, a business contract, or, at worst, a friend. But those losses are easier to recoup than a loss of self-esteem. You have to trust your internal navigation system, and if something really doesn't feel right, knowing that you have the power of two feet and can walk away from any deal gives you the strength to stand behind your convictions.

(As a side note, try not to make these big decisions on a Friday, because then you have the entire weekend to ruminate about whether or not you did the right thing.)

When something doesn't feel right and you do change your mind, that's empowering, and you will be more self-confident the next go-round. A deal is a deal only if both parties agree it's in their mutual best interests. If one person feels taken advantage of or pushed into it, then neither one of you is going to be happy in the end.

80. Friends as Family

In everyone's life, at some time, our inner fire goes out. It is then burst into flame by an encounter with another human being. We should all be thankful for those people who rekindle the inner spirit.

—Albert Schweitzer

Millions of people feel lonely every day—many for good reason. They may be separated from their loved ones, or their family may have passed away. A few, by choice, isolate themselves in order to find some inner peace. For all who suffer this kind of loneliness, self-confidence is shaken to its core.

Some people opt out of their families of origin due to abuse or neglect. This is an act of self-preservation, and a necessity for survival, but it's still hard and lonely. If life has forced you to walk away from your relatives, take heart. You are not alone.

Whether the circumstances occurred by nature or by choice, the result and cure are the same: For many people, building a family of friends is an appropriate thing to do. Having a close and loving group of friends who are supportive and able to be there for you is a blessing. These relationships require the same level of commitment and trust any successful family needs to thrive.

You may have heard that married people live longer than single people. Indeed, studies on longevity show that those who live alone die sooner than those who live with others, but it has little to do with being married. The key is being involved with other human beings.

Being involved means bonding with others and filling your life with people and activities that give you the sense that you are part of something larger than yourself. Being with other people gives you something you can rarely get by yourself: validation.

Long-term friendships become more important in time because the process of sharing your history with other people creates a powerful connection. It seems that when people who knew each other in school reunite, relationships are potent. This goes for romantic connections as well as friendships.

Making new friends helps us to live longer and keeps Alzheimer's at bay, for it causes our minds to think and feel in new ways. Every time we do something differently, we reinforce connections in our brains. New relationships require that we take in new information, process it, and try to achieve a desired result.

If you want to be friends with someone, it's usually pretty easy, for, most of the time, we like people who like us. By asking nonthreatening questions, you can show an interest in someone you are trying to get to know. You can share your thoughts and opinions on movies, books, and newspaper columns, or experience a new restaurant together.

When you create a family of friends, know that these are the people you have chosen to be in your circle. Do everything you can to honor their participation, and you will find solace in their presence. Remember that you have to *be* a friend to make a friend.

81. Recognize Your Abilities

*If you hear a voice within you say "you cannot paint,"
then by all means paint, and that voice will be silenced.*
—Vincent Van Gogh

The number-one motivator of people is recognition. Saying to a teammate that you recognize her efforts to make your working relationship great is the best motivator you could give to her. Letting someone you love know that he has added to your life by being himself is one of the highest compliments you can pay. Many people fall short by not giving some of that recognition to themselves as well.

If we could only realize who we truly are and give ourselves credit for being our best selves. This is especially important when we're not feeling it. Once you know what you're capable of, it's hard to feel good when you fall short, but you have to keep those setbacks in perspective. Truly confident people recognize that they have succeeded in the past and still have the ability to do it again—and will.

Knowing that you have talent and really taking that in will help you get through almost any situation. Believing in yourself requires that you are able to recognize what your abilities are and pat yourself on the back for having them. This isn't ego-tripping; it's a necessity for integrating confidence-boosting behaviors into your thought process and lifestyle.

So the next time you have a win, do something you're proud of, or make a good point, silently recognize that you have done well, and feel good about it. It makes you better at being your best self.

82. Determination Is the Key

I am convinced all of humanity is born with more gifts than we know. Most are born geniuses and just get de-geniused rapidly.
—Buckminster Fuller

Life is difficult, and the greatest accomplishments are filled with the greatest rewards precisely because they are difficult. In practicing determination, you will develop your abilities to not only deal with the adversity in front of you, but also to thrive while you are doing it.

Psychologist Dr. Stephen Trudeau says it this way: "We need determination to keep at it when there is resistance to our efforts." And he should know; in addition to being a busy therapist he is also the author of *The Special Needs of Parenting*, which was inspired by his and his wife Mary's joys and challenges with their son Devin, who has cerebral palsy.

I admire Dr. Trudeau for many reasons. He and Mary knew that their son wouldn't be "normal," and they were even told that he would never know their names or be able to communicate, and that he wouldn't be able to live a full life. But they were determined to have their baby and make the best of it.

The early years were a huge struggle, with multiple surgeries, which continue to this day. It has to be one of the hardest things in the world, watching your child in pain and frightened by hospitals, doctors, shots, and all those strange tests. This family hung together, and their love has grown along with their determination to provide a future for their son.

Today, Devin is an active pre-teen who, though he must use a walker, totally takes life as it comes. Though he can't play sports with other kids, he is able to ride in his dad's motorcycle's sidecar, and it does get its fair share of attention.

When they come to Uncle Barton's, Devin likes to walk up and down the stairs, and, though he takes his time, he is determined to make it on his own, and he does. He's still a kid and is as obstinate as they all can be. He's also learned not to see his handicap as a stop sign. Devin figures out ways around obstacles, and sometimes that requires a little assistance from an adult, but he holds his own. He has even mastered piloting an electric boat and takes his captain's duties very seriously, making sure everyone remains seated and there's no horseplay.

The determination to keep going in the face of multiple challenges has helped the whole family. You can call it whatever you like, but the point is that, despite the setbacks, this family is thriving in the face of difficulty. Their confidence is strong, as is their bond. When a person is determined, a lot can be accomplished. When a family shares that determination as part of their value system the positive results are multiplied.

If your confidence is shaken because you or members of your family are struggling, take heart in the Trudeaus' story. You need to believe that no matter what you are facing you have the determination and the confidence to get through it, and lead a full and fun life.

83. Give Up Lying

I cannot tell a lie...I did it with my little hatchet.
—George Washington

Not many among us willingly admit to lying. So why give it up? Because lying robs us of our dignity. When we lie, we may feel we have gotten out of trouble or impressed somebody with our tale, but all we have really done is erode our own self-esteem and confidence. By lying we attack our own credibility with our words and deeds.

Lying comes in many forms. Defensive lying is meant to keep us from taking responsibility, or for getting us out of trouble. There are also lies meant to embellish the truth to make us appear more impressive or involved than we are. Perhaps the most common form is lying to avoid hurting others' feelings. Too bad we are so creative about how many ways we can be untruthful.

Sometimes our lies, untruths, and embellishments come back to haunt us. As the lies build so does the need to keep lying to support the original lies. Soon enough one is caught in a web so sticky that the pressure of all the lies is strangling. When you start to feel that you have told too many lies, it's time to come clean. It is also wise to remember here that confession can be good for the soul.

But what is a lie? Many people use, as an operating definition, something similar to not telling the truth, or telling an untruth. But these definitions are left over from the simplistic explanations of our childhood. The best description of a lie I have ever heard is this: telling an untruth or omitting the truth to someone who *deserves* to know the truth.

Who decides who deserves to know the truth? You do. You do this by being honest with yourself and being dedicated to living an ethical life. Trust me, you can do this. Let me give an example of this concept in action. If a stranger asks me how much money I have in the bank, I am under no obligation to tell him, because he does not deserve to know the truth. It is none of his business. However, if my wife asks me where I spent my afternoon this past Friday after work, I tell her exactly what, why, where, and with whom because she does deserve to know the truth, and I love her.

People often bring up the circumstance of needing to tell a "white lie," and it should be obvious that there is no need to be so truthful that you hurt other people.

If my grandmother is wearing an ugly dress that she is very proud of, I will tell her she looks lovely, because it serves no useful purpose to destroy her good feelings.

Get rid of the lies about how magnificent, athletic, lucky, or amazing you are. Believe it or not, exactly who you are is interesting enough. Besides, most people don't believe you anyway. Bragging lies and embellishments are usually pretty obvious. Stick to the honest truth about yourself, and you might be surprised how much people like the actual you!

Lying creates unneeded stress. Developing the habit of telling the truth is liberating. By not having to waste precious brain space on remembering which lies and embellishments were told to whom, you begin to feel more calm, relaxed, and less stressed.

Getting rid of the defensive lie is the most liberating of all. When you are caught or cornered by not living up to your employment contract, then the best defense is to admit your mistake and vow to take corrective action immediately. When we lie defensively to cover up our errors, sooner or later it catches up with us. Better to be known not as the perfect person, but rather the person who has flaws but is willing to change them.

By getting rid of the lies in your life, you will gain a sense of peace and confidence—the confidence in knowing that you have nothing to hide, nothing to fear. You will sleep very well with no lies on your conscience.

This chapter was coauthored by Dr. Stephen Trudeau (www.humansguide.com).

84. Sticks and Stones

No one can make you feel inferior without your permission.
—Eleanor Roosevelt

What others think of you is none of your business, and you should not allow it to influence your self-concept. Being dispassionate when it comes to critical comments (or rumors) from those around you is a great tool for success and maintaining your self-confidence.

The reality here is that no two people can live or work together without occasionally stepping on each other's toes. If someone does you wrong, it most likely wasn't intentional, and if it was, that could be a signal that you may need to move on, or at least get some kind of coaching or counseling.

If you allow yourself to get twisted by the uninformed or just plain unkind words of a person who could be either jealous or insecure, your life will become unpleasant, and your confidence level will drop like a stone. Remember what your mom said when you were teased as a child: consider the source. And then there's the old "sticks and stones" line.

The truth is that the negative things people may say about you come from their own discomfort and inner turmoil. If someone is acting in a passive-aggressive manner in order to get your goat (or make you look bad) and you let her know she has gotten to you, it will encourage her to do it again. By ignoring her inappropriate and inaccurate comments or actions, you take away her power. Personally I think of such people as troubled souls, and simply move on.

People in a position of power are generally aware of these bad behaviors in the workplace, and take blamers and rumor mongers with a large grain of salt. But if you let them affect your performance or mood, you can confuse those around you. I know it can be a real challenge to not get offended or angry at a person who has said or done something that caused you pain, but by taking this advice you are actually protecting yourself in the event that any other similar incidence should occur.

You also build your inner strength and reinforce your self-confidence by responding rather than reacting to a remark. Refraining from showing your ire at being offended is a sign that you're above it. Projecting that kind of self-esteem will make you immune to the inappropriate, critical comments of those who would like to see you fail. It then becomes a waste of their time and energy.

If you just let negative comments roll off your back, the offender will stop. If the behavior continues, a one-to-one discussion is in order, but if that doesn't work, bring in a third party from outside of your relationship or job. I believe that you can choose the best course of action based on the seriousness of the offense, but don't go for the throat because that lowers you to the offender's level.

By maintaining your dignity and not allowing yourself to become offended, your self-confidence remains intact, you keep your focus, and you maintain the respect of those around you. And I truly believe that is your best course of action.

85. Tiny Bright Spots

To believe your own thought, to believe that what is true for you in our private heart is for all men—that is genius.
—Ralph Waldo Emerson

Sometimes all we need to get through a difficult time is tiny bit of brightness in our lives—getting that parking place right in front of the store, unexpectedly finding a $20 bill in the pocket of your jeans, or seeing a wisp of joy in the eyes of a loved one. Little things like these can make a big difference in your day.

It may be hard to hold on to the feeling for long, but that's okay. If you're going through a rough patch, it's quite healthy for you to come out of it for just a minute or two. We all know that staying stressed or depressed is not good for our well-being, so just allowing yourself to experience a positive emotion, even momentary happiness in the midst of chaos, will help you maintain some energy and get you closer to healing your issue.

If you take a break from your troubles, even a very small one, you can't help but look at things differently. Yes, the problem will still be there, but it won't be as overwhelming as it was. Knowing that you can smile or have a laugh while you're battling your demons is very empowering. But often, those moments are elusive, so you have to get good at looking for them.

People who have pets they love can usually get a few seconds of lightness by seeing their animals happy. Whether at rest or play, our four-legged friends can give us a little lift in even the darkest times. I have recommended that many people rescue a dog or cat because I know that, in almost all cases, the person benefits as much as (if not more than) the pet.

Going for a walk or looking at a picturesque view, even if you have to drive to a place you find inspiring, is very healing. While taking your constitutional, look around and absorb as much of the beauty as you can. Making the effort to fill your mind and heart will help you see that, although it may be a dark time, there are rays of sunshine out there.

When little things go well, when we are in the company of friends and family, or when we accomplish even a small task, our psyche gets a positive charge that can help us lighten up. Finding ways to brighten your life is something all of us can get better at. Don't fool yourself; everyone (even Oprah) goes through difficult times. Those of us who are practiced at it have learned to celebrate the small victories.

Finding those tiny bright spots may not seem like much, but give it a try and be open to being lifted out of your pit. It can only happen one step at a time.

86. Dealing With Disappointment

*Age does not diminish the extreme disappointment
of having a scoop of ice cream fall from the cone.*
—Jim Fiebig

Sometimes things just don't work out. In your world, Murphy's Law may seem to be the way of things, and you feel disillusioned with your life and perhaps yourself.

Dealing with disappointment is something most people don't think self-confident people ever have to cope with. The real truth is that everyone deals with disappointment differently; those who embrace confident behaviors may not be thrown off course as easily as someone who has a fair amount of self-doubt. The good news is that anyone can learn how to get better at handling disappointment, and as you do, the secondary benefit is that you increase your self-confidence.

For the disappointed, their reactions can be anything from taking to their beds for days on end (not terribly practical if you have a life), to perhaps getting down on themselves and stifling their productivity. When you take a disappointment and turn it against yourself, or blame yourself for it, the results are going to be emotional pain and a loss of energy.

We all need to find our own ways of coping with life when things don't go in the direction we want them to. From failed relationships to missed business opportunities or financial losses, this is the stuff life is made of. If you pull the covers up over your head, you'll never have the opportunity to use your disappointment to get to the next level, or at the very least, to learn from it.

An aware individual feels the normal sadness that accompanies a setback; a self-confident one lets the feelings out constructively, and also makes a plan to help himself feel better. This usually involves some kind of emotional or physical release such as working in the house or yard, seeing a therapist, exercising, or anything that allows one to let go and thereby process his feelings. This is followed by some kind of action to help balance out the dissatisfaction.

You may not be able to fix the initial disappointment, but you can put energy into other things and make yourself feel better by getting something constructive accomplished. No matter what is going on in your world, cleaning out your sock drawer, pruning the roses, or writing the next great American novel is going to make you feel better about yourself and your situation.

Disappointment takes the wind out of our sails. You can sit, becalmed, in the middle of your regret, or you can choose to get out your paddle and start working your way to shore. Whether you end up on a deserted island or a tropical paradise I can't say. But staying where you are will surely turn you into fish food, so the only real choice is to start rowing.

Being momentarily disenchanted with your circumstances is totally human. Staying in that place is a choice—pure and simple. I would rather fail a hundred times than never try. Life is too short to live with disappointment, and there are so many ways to make things happen. You can do it.

87. Perfection Will Come in Time

Certain flaws are necessary for the whole. It would seem strange if old friends lacked certain quirks.
—Goethe

When people ask me how to write, I tell them to just throw up on paper. That may be a little graphic, but the idea is just to write down what's in your head. Getting it out on paper may lead you in a new direction, give you additional material you didn't even know you had, and also make you feel as though you've accomplished something. Having an entire page filled with your words is a great confidence-builder.

Experience has taught me that the best way to get something done is just to sit down and get started. When I begin, I'm not striving for perfection; I just want to reach the finish line. Not every chapter is brilliant, but the good news is that I can refine it later if I like—that's what editing is for. The important thing for me is to write as often as possible. The old saying about slow and steady winning the race works in my world, and it can in yours as well. The difference here is that I'm not worried about how I look while I'm heading toward my goal because I know I can tune things up later.

I began my writing career with a monthly column, and then I started writing a different weekly column. At first I was worried that I couldn't pull off writing two columns, but after a little while it became part of my routine. Then I took on my first book project. It was a bit of a challenge, but I was able to integrate the work into my day, and now I actually look forward to my "writing hour." You are currently reading the fourth book I've written using this process.

The idea is to learn that getting started is the second-hardest part—staying on task for many days in a row is much more challenging. And needing perfection right off the bat will slow you down to a crawl.

To get things rolling, it works best to lay out a framework or outline and some kind of a time line. Stick to it as much as possible, and don't worry about getting everything right the first time around. Just make sure you give yourself enough space to refine your work if necessary. Some people are talented enough that their first attempts are usually pretty good. Even if that's not you, remember that the more you try the better you are going to get.

Don't get me wrong; I love perfection, I just don't need it on my first attempts. Going for perfection impedes creativity. Give your project your whole heart and mind, and whatever comes out is going to be quality work, and it's also going to be something you will be proud of.

88. Don't Allow Age to Intimidate You

As a man grows older it is harder
and harder to frighten him.
—Jean Paul Richter

I saw a sign at Knott's Berry Farm when I was a teenager that read, "Don't regret growing older; there are few people who have that privilege." I have always remembered it and kept it as part of my value system. It helps me enjoy my time on the planet with few regrets, and also gives me a confident attitude about the future.

Everybody had to be born sometime, and if you don't like your age, that negativity will trickle down into other areas of your life and chip away at your self-esteem. Look, you are who you are, and you are the age you are. Accepting that is the only way to have a fulfilled life. If you mourn your youth, you don't get to savor the moment, the confidence that comes with experience, or the wisdom that accompanies age.

James Taylor once sang, "The secret of life is enjoying the passage of time," and I couldn't agree more. I'm sure there's more than one secret, but this one's a goodie. If you can't love each day, and squeeze as much out of it as you are able, then you will go to sleep with regrets and wake up with anxiety. Trusting that you are in the right place, at the right age, with the right people will give you more joy and confidence than a room full of self-help CDs.

I don't want to be a dysfunctional old man. I want a "good enough" quality of life. I say it that way because I know that age can have some drawbacks, and I hate being disappointed, so I like to keep my expectations reasonable. I imagine I will have a few physical issues, and they may slow me down, but I won't let them stop me. Besides, isn't slowing down the best way to see the world around you?

The truth is that no one gets out of here alive, and you just have to choose to make the best of where you are right now. If you don't, the joy you could be feeling will turn into woulda-shoulda-couldas, and you will be emotionally uncomfortable, no matter what your age.

Be who you are and what you are. I love seeing men wear T-shirts that say things like "Old Guys Rule!" Not only are the dudes sporting them taking life with a grain of salt and saying "I may be older, but I don't act like it," but they also have the sense of humor necessary to get them out of bed every day.

I know too many people whose lives, loves, and careers didn't begin until they were in their 40s or 50s, and they're getting way more out of the second half of life. Please know that you could also be that person.

89. Trying Too Hard

We can disagree, without being disagreeable.
—Barack Obama

Confidence has to come from a positive place, not from insecurity or neurosis. Those behaviors may appear confident to the outside world—at least for the first five minutes—but will never be real confidence. People who are truly impressive never have to *try* to appear that way.

If you don't have anything to prove, and hold no false pretenses, that is real confidence. People give respect because they want to, not because they have to. If you aren't honest about who you are, the people who you want to be supportive won't be willing (or even know how) to support you. You will never have the relationships you want unless you drop your pretenses. This is not weakness; you are not showing your vulnerabilities. You are opening yourself up to being your true self and to growing as a person. Dishonesty or just plain BS will never get you where you want to go. If you openly share your intentions, you will be able to move forward, work with anyone, and succeed together.

Graciousness, a sense of community, and being willing to admit who you really are—those are the keys to confidence. Learn to appreciate what everyone brings to the table, including yourself, and in the nicest way possible, share your ideas. When you do, everyone grows.

90. Never Let School Get in the Way of Your Education

Nothing is a waste of time if you use the experience wisely.
—Auguste Rodin

When I was a child, my parents took me out of school to travel with them. My father believed that the things I was exposed to were more educational than anything I could get from a classroom. I can't say I disagree. I have always felt that I could deal with any situation because I experienced many different ones in the process of growing up simply because my parents dragged me around the country.

The idea of taking kids out of school to travel is generally met with gasps of horror: "They will miss their assignments, they will never catch up, and they need their peer support." All are valid concerns, but these days there are so many techno tools that can keep you connected, as well as the option of homeschooling, that traveling with your family when most everyone else is at home can be a bonding (as well as an educational) experience. That bond is actually very important to fostering confidence in both your child and yourself as a parent. If you know you are doing the absolute best for your child, you are going to feel better about yourself. No question.

One of my teachers, Mrs. Tiger (see, we all remember them), encouraged us to help others and get involved in what she called "social action" as a group. The dynamics of teamwork, the knowledge that accompanies travel, and the understanding of different people from different places can be more enlightening than college. The confidence that came with our actions, although a bunch of fifth graders could hardly change the world, certainly changed me and added to the fabric of my life.

I know families who homeschool their children while they are on the road. The kids I know who "go to school" on the sets of television shows and movies are usually ahead of their classmates when they return to regular school. And most of the people I know who have been educated in other countries have a different attitude toward their matriculation. They want to learn and be the best they can because they have seen and done things that inspired them to reach for the brass ring and keep up-leveling their lives.

By the way, traveling, homeschooling parents are also learning, growing, and getting the warmth that comes from knowing that they are doing the best things possible to raise confident children.

91. Finding the Best in Others

I have found the paradox that if I love until it hurts, then there is no hurt, but only more love.
—Mother Teresa

My friend Dan Maddux—let's call him a Meetings Entrepreneur—began a new project just before the Great Recession. His vision was to open a 30,000-square-foot convention facility in Las Vegas called "MEET."

Though exposed to the ugliest side of life with the financial crisis, he would not let the project fail. At a time when the financial landscape of the city was a desert, he had the confidence necessary to keep things moving forward. Dan's first financial partner was unable to continue to fund the project, but Dan and his team stayed the course and found a new banker who really believed in his vision and business plan.

Maddux shared with me that "In a good economy anyone can make money. Finding the strength to continue in a down time isn't easy. I had my doubts early on, but I learned a lot from previous bad situations and I didn't want to experience it again. I can look back on the year and see it as an education."

I asked him about holding large meetings at a time when most everyone is cutting back, and his response was quintessential: "The real buyers are still there, it's there, and without the looky-loos, the lower attendance actually makes for a better show because it gives exhibitors the time to focus on their best clients and most likely business contacts. We count on diversity, and, while many places are finding business going away, we are still doing business as usual, despite what the press may be saying about the demise of Las Vegas." Vegas is well-positioned for the fastest recovery when compared to its competition.

Keeping things in perspective and not allowing the fear to take hold is an important factor in Dan's success. He also keeps his eye on the future. When he thinks back on how it all happened he remembers that when he first entered the workforce he wasn't confident, but did have several competencies, which he focused on. Instead of looking at what he didn't have or what others had more of, he said to himself, "Wow, I'm not ugly or stupid" (messages from childhood). He realized that he worked twice as hard to keep people from seeing the flaws he thought he had, and realized that he was more creative and resourceful than most. He dropped the idea of being the best at everything, and instead he decided it was okay to find people who had competencies he lacked.

"Having someone join me who has a talent I do not have doesn't threaten me, it enhances me," says Dan, and the converse is also true: "Some of the best lessons I've learned were from people who were the worst human beings possible. I saw bad behaviors and challenged myself to see how I could do it differently. It gave me insight I needed to succeed."

One of the tools Dan uses is not merely interviewing people for an hour—he takes three, because he believes that anyone can be good for an hour, but you really see who a person is after two or more. "You can do wonderful things with someone who is right," Maddux says. "If we engage people who are not simpatico and can't be creative or don't have good intentions, it can cripple our business, so we only work with individuals who we resonate with and who can rise above their own issues and stay open to getting the best out of people by helping them understand the nature or culture of how we think."

He goes on to say:

You can perceive [people] as competent because they are arrogant or bulldozers. Truly competent people don't have those kinds of behaviors. Those false confidence behaviors are only a mask and you have to learn how to navigate around it, but it's best to avoid it. I didn't let those behaviors infect me. Strangely, I see more of the negative from people who have reached the pinnacle of success rather than those who are starting out.

Knowing yourself and how the world perceives you and being aware enough to see how people can make judgments, breaking through to the positive side of things is the best way to win their favor and understanding. People feel a difference when you communicate by seeing what's whole and good and honest and appreciating it. I try to guide my people and say that we're all selling something, so get back to the core of customer service, like a proper greeting. If someone throws you a negative curve, but you are able to focus on the likable qualities, it will make the conversation or the deal much easier for both of you.

Dan recommends to:

Try to be nice to everybody, especially to service people or those who are there for your safety, like airline personnel. You never know when you're going to run into someone who knows you. The higher level you are in more people are watching you, so being your best self will keep others from misunderstanding what you're about. It's also wise to learn to discuss uncomfortable issues with a smile on your face, because others are always aware. People love to see other people's trainwrecks, and I don't want anyone to see us as anything but a comprehensive team.

If you really want to read people, don't judge them when they have the floor; look at them when they are relating without attention from other people. You will then know who they really are and can delve into what's important, and [that] will help you get the most out of them.

Dan's advice is an important piece in the development of self-confidence. He has won several awards because of his accomplishments as well as his understanding of people at all levels of business and society.

92. Act "As If"

You cannot consistently perform in a manner which is inconsistent with the way you see yourself.
—Zig Ziglar

Acting as though life is already going your way can be a great psychological tool for building confidence. It allows you to physically and emotionally feel success in your body. You also send out a vibe others pick up.

We've all heard the clichés "Fake it 'til you make it" and "See it then be it," and as with all old sayings they must have come from someone's (and then many people's) experience. Hey, if it works, why not give it a try?

I think it's easy to confuse "acting as if" and being a phony. "Acting as if" doesn't mean that you pretend to be something you're not and rack up tens of thousands of dollars in credit card debt. It is about using the power of your emotions to get things in your life flowing in the direction you would like them to.

For example, if you want to be an executive, start behaving like one. Dress in appropriate business attire, get up early and plan your day, make the necessary prospecting and follow-up phone calls—even though you may be doing it all from your home office. Quite simply, acting as though you have a full-time job will make it easier for you to get one because you're used to putting in a full day and behaving as a success.

In addition, you are putting to use the "power of intention," which was reprised to the world in the best-selling book *The Secret* and championed by New Thought leaders such as Dr. Wayne Dyer. *Intention* refers to keeping your goal in mind as part of your daily routine. The best way to do that is to constantly keep a mental picture in your mind and in your heart of what you want and where you want to be. I believe that the emotional component is the most important part, because this process creates a type of imprinting on your brain, which makes it easier to reach your goals because they will feel completely natural.

Imagine feeling as though you are supposed to be in the corner office—not in an entitled way, but in the way you act when you are feeling truly self-confident about who you are. It's an inner knowing that can only come from trusting your intuition and believing in yourself.

That quiet confidence may be more powerful than an MBA when it comes to getting to where you want to go.

93. Change Your Thinking

Do not let what you cannot do interfere with what you can do.
—John Wooden

Changing the way you think can be very healthy. Unfortunately, sometimes it takes a painful loss, such as suddenly being laid off or having your partner leave you, to do it. After something of that magnitude occurs, you are compelled to look at your life differently. Making a significant transformation in your life, such as getting clean and sober, also requires the rewiring of your thought processes.

What happens then is you create new, more positive pathways in your brain, and that changes the way you think and feel for the better because you then process your thoughts and emotions in an alternate manner. If you try to ignore the changes in your thinking, you will not be able to sustain your transition, bring in new relationships, or open up new opportunities.

These adjustments are only possible if you find the will to look at life from a different perspective. Understanding that your old way of thinking may actually be holding you back can be a big motivator.

Making the choice to create a better life for yourself and for those you love is something that comes from being self-confident and knowing that it's time to make an adjustment. And even if it is a very personal action, it inevitably involves others, especially when it is something like changing the way you communicate or learning how to fight fairly and controlling your temper, which may require some instruction or counseling.

If you want to make a change, the support of friends and family can be critical. Set aside some time to reinforce your relationships so that you can get the assistance you desire. You may need to risk asking some difficult questions if you want to get clarity about what your loved ones see in you. People who are alone can find it much more difficult to make mental and emotional shifts.

Once you discover that your old way of being is no longer working, and you're struggling to figure out how to change, a support group can be helpful. The folks there can assist you by explaining and modeling new behaviors, and you can also learn things about yourself that may be difficult to see without an outside perspective. Just be aware that not everyone in every group has it together, and you need to be careful in selecting people to sponsor or mentor you.

Most of us know that life is full of changes. We usually adapt pretty well to things around us—or even other people—changing. It can be a lot harder when we are the ones who need to make the move to a new way of living our lives. Trust that you did not come to this decision lightly. Even if it's something you initially didn't want to do, once you see the necessity, it will be easier to get on board.

Whatever your needs are, remember that it all starts with you, and making important changes is truly a gift you are giving to yourself and to the ones who care for you.

94. Rituals of Achievement

The human race advances only by the extra achievements of the individual. You are the individual.
—Charles Towne

The caps and gowns are pressed, the diplomas are printed, and families are gathering from around the country to celebrate as their loved one steps into a new world. Graduating from high school, college, or another educational program is both a culmination of time well spent and a beginning of the next stage of life. Receiving that diploma is one of the most confidence-boosting experiences anyone can have.

Rituals of achievement have always been around in one form or another. Whether spiritually or educationally, the day someone leaves one world and enters another is something to be celebrated.

Graduations are an important rite of passage. Taking that walk, receiving a degree, and slowly reading every word printed on it gives you or your child a sense of pride that can be truly life-changing. To have embarked on and completed such a challenging journey is an experience that will serve anyone through the rest of her life.

Some who are graduating will be leaving the nest. As a parent, you may want to encourage your children to take stock of what it took to get them there by reminding them to reflect on the past as they look toward the future.

If your kids (or you) are graduating from college, they are now officially becoming adults. Most will enter the workforce, some will go on to graduate school, and others will choose to travel. In some way, they are all moving to another level in their lives. It's both exciting and scary.

I think we have two jobs as parents. The first is to teach our children to be kind to one another. The second is to teach them how to live without us. And sometimes life itself is not so kind. All parents hope for the same things at their child's graduation: They hope that their children have learned how to deal with this complicated thing we call life; they hope that their children are at least somewhat prepared to be let loose into the real world, where they will be making their own decisions and reaping the results.

Graduation is a time that is full of hope, and it's important to acknowledge this moment. I suggest celebrating your child's graduation as a family event. Make it a shared experience you will all remember the rest of your lives. Life doesn't give us that many opportunities to relish in something that is almost always joyful. Any time you get a chance to create a wonderful memory, take it.

One final tip: Whenever you or anyone you care for receives a diploma, whether it be from elementary or graduate school, have it nicely framed as soon as possible and get it up on the wall. It will serve as a reminder of a significant accomplishment and as an inspiration to accomplish more.

A friend of mine called to invite me to her son's graduation—from kindergarten. The whole clan is flying in. Even though this may seem a little over the top, any time a loving family can get together and share in a celebration of achieving a goal, it strengthens the ties that bind. And that in itself is a confidence-builder.

95. Feelings Aren't Facts

When dealing with people, remember you are not dealing with creatures of logic, but creatures of emotion.
—Dale Carnegie

Emotions are at the core of our motivation and our confidence, and they are why we continue on with life even in the face of disappointment or disaster. You may know many emotional people, and you may be one yourself—it's not a bad thing. Moreover, as a psychotherapist (and a human being), I believe that emotions are a *good* thing.

Throughout the years many of us learn to accept, enjoy, understand, and trust our feelings. After all, it worked very well for Luke Skywalker. And who would want to give up all those warm fuzzies? The problem is that sometimes we only feel the cold prickly ones, those that are scary or painful, and that undermines our sense of self. Understanding that it is possible that our own emotions are not telling us the truth helps with the healing.

Upon occasion some people get a feeling that isn't real. They may think it's real, it may feel very real, and he or she may truly *believe* it's real, but it's just a feeling. It is wise to remember that, as important as emotions are, feelings aren't facts.

Many things make us feel. Some are happening right now, others are from our past, and some things that cause many people to be destabilized are in the uncertain future. Still other emotions are mere fantasies, lies we tell ourselves that make us needlessly unhappy, or misunderstandings. There is no end to the amount of feeling (both positive and negative) that flows through our lives on a daily basis; the trick is to learn how to differentiate between feelings that are born out of our imagination and those that are real and verifiable.

Just because your boss or your partner looked at you in a funny way or spoke with a sharp tone doesn't mean that he is mad at you. He could be rushed or having a bad moment, or you could be misinterpreting the message. Unfortunately, you could have misinterpreted and be feeling horrible about an imagined negative outcome. Then you can walk around for days thinking that you are in trouble or that your life, as you know it, is over. It doesn't have to be that way.

The best thing to do when you are feeling as though something isn't right is to check it out. Don't sit on it, push it down, or try to ignore it; your emotions won't cooperate. Sometimes the only way out is by getting into the feelings and first looking at how you might be creating them. Combine that with some gentle (not accusatory) questioning of the person or people who you believe may be the cause. Look for truth and be open to see how it's possible that your feelings may not be accurate. Of course, it can also be helpful to get an outside perspective from someone you trust is on your team, and from whom you can hear the truth. It can be as simple as asking, "Are we okay?"

This process isn't an easy one, but it is far less painful than living your life feeling as though your world is crashing in on you.

96. Taking Risks Shows Strength

You'll always miss 100 percent of the shots you don't take.
—Wayne Gretzky

Keep your expectations low and you won't get disappointed—but you won't get much else either. Yes, it's emotionally safer to have preferences instead of expectations, or not to expect much from yourself or others, but what does that really get you?

Dealing appropriately with disappointment is different from setting yourself up for them. A setup might be auditioning for *American Idol* when you've never successfully performed for the public: Not only will you be disappointed, but you could also be humiliated in front of millions of people (which might lead you to seeking solace in the bottom of a Haagen-Dazs container).

Appropriately dealing with disappointment doesn't mean you can't sulk a little; it's natural to reevaluate after a disheartening experience. It also doesn't mean you have to suck it up and put on a happy face when you feel like crawling into a hole. It *does* mean that you have to learn from your encounter and take steps to make the next one better. It also helps to keep things in perspective, which may mean simply believing that there will *be* a next time.

What you have to remember is that when you put yourself out there, whether it be for love or performing in front of the world, you are taking the risk of your "audience" not responding the way you would like. You also have to remember that few people take risks, and being able to do so says something wonderful about you.

A brave person is not one who rushes into battle without the thought of serious injury or death; it's the one who is frightened but marches forward anyway. That is true courage. It may take a good friend or a loved one to point out to you that, even though things didn't go quite how you would have liked, you have accomplished something huge and should be proud of yourself.

The problem for some people is that, if their dream doesn't work out the first time they try for it, they usually settle for something less. That may not be a bad thing; a good experience is worth its weight in gold—but a great experience is priceless. Moreover, if you don't at least reach for the brass ring, you will always wonder what life might have been like had you made the attempt, and succeeded. So don't settle, and don't give up.

97. The Sum Total

Do not be too timid and squeamish about your actions.
All life is an experiment. The more
experiments you make the better.
What if they are a little coarse, and you
may get your coat soiled or torn?
What if you do fail, and get fairly
rolled in the dirt once or twice.
Up again, you shall never be so afraid of a tumble.
—Ralph Waldo Emerson

You are the sum total of your experiences, and the end result of your time here on Earth could be far different from what you imagine. Whether you believe you are headed for greatness or anonymity, life has a way of making you change your direction despite anything and everything you do to stop it.

Self-confident people understand that there are inevitable twists and turns on the road to creating what you want. They learn to go with the flow and not give too much significance to any one particular event. That's a pretty enlightened view, one that is practical and does work. All you have to do is learn the technique (and continue to practice) and you will be able to change your thinking pattern.

If you see yourself as a failure because you've been divorced, fired, or in some other way summarily dumped, it has to be looked at as one event and not a prison sentence. Just because one person or company didn't want you doesn't mean that several others won't. Again, it's just plain common sense, but we do like to wallow in our losses, and that act just erodes your self-esteem like rust on a garden tool.

Train your brain to think about something that inspires you every time you recognize that you are thinking about something that holds you back. This simple action will change your life and the way you look at it.

Another tool you can use when your mind wanders into dangerous waters is to focus on what you do best. Whether it's playing golf, running a company, or just running your mouth, start giving your talent focus. You will instantly begin producing chemicals (such as serotonin) in your brain that will lighten your mood and help you create a more confident mindset.

Just because you have lost the game a few times doesn't mean you can't make a comeback, no matter how late in the season. Self-confidence gives us the ability to keep forging ahead, even if we've had a bad year—or even several of them.

98. Try Puppy Love

You think dogs will not be in heaven?
I tell you, they will be there long before any of us.
—Robert Louis Stevenson

A couple of years ago I started looking for a new partner in my counseling practice—I wanted to rescue and train a therapy dog.

I know of a very few respected therapists who practice with their dogs to add a broader scope to their work, and the idea has merit. For someone in emotional distress who is unable to open up and let the pain out, being in the presence of a furry and unconditionally loving creature can be very helpful.

In addition, there are a number of organizations with volunteers who escort gentle and friendly animals to convalescent homes and hospitals. These loving creatures bring real emotional healing to those who are infirm.

I was a bit hesitant about this adoption, knowing the pros and cons (such as replacing the carpet and never again having matching slippers). But the pros won out; the dog could help my clients. I also liked the idea of having someone to take walks with when no humans were available.

This little bundle of fluff has brought a new dimension of love into my life and into the lives of everyone she touches. I don't bring her to every session, because for some people it's not appropriate (such as those who are allergic or canine-phobic), but I'd be hard-pressed to even think of being without her. Even my 15-year-old cat has accepted the little Yorkshire terrorist.

When I tell Mercy that she's going to work, she gets very excited. When she gets together with people she's familiar with, it's like they have never been separated. She sits in their lap or at their feet, simply adding comfort where she can.

I recently met an elderly woman who was walking her little Yorkie, and, as the doggies sniffed each other, she told me that instead of sending flowers after her husband died several years ago, her children all chipped in and got her a puppy, along with a cell phone. She was concerned at first, but having to care for the dog helped her to heal and made her take walks, and now the dog is her constant companion. She says it saved her life and gave her the confidence to move forward, even though the future was uncertain.

The bond we share with animals is amazing. For some, it even replaces the need for human companionship: Think of the little old lady with a house full of cats or the bachelor with his faithful dog. Years ago, I heard about an aging couple who committed suicide together after the loss of their pet—a tragic decision; instead, they could have rescued an animal that would have rescued them right back.

In many ways, caring for an animal makes you more human. Doing it as a family teaches your children responsibility and helps everyone involved experience the circle of life.

So, if someone you care for wants to bring a sock-stealing poop machine into your world, give it some thought. The truth is, we can always replace shoes, but we never seem to have enough love in our lives.

If you are interested in rescuing an animal you can go to your local shelter, or call 1-800-SAVE-A-PET, or go online to www.1-800-save-a-pet.com.

99. On the Same Page With the Opposite Sex

The Constitution only guarantees the American people the right to pursue happiness. You have to catch it yourself.
—Benjamin Franklin

Recent research by *The Journal of Happiness Studies* discovered that men and women differ greatly in their happiest—and therefore most confident—years. The survey concluded that men tend to be less happy when they are younger (in their 20s and 30s), when women are at their happiest. Then, when we turn 48, so do the tables. Men tend to get happier as they age, and women tend to become less so. Makes you wonder if the genders will ever be on the same page for more than a nanosecond.

Although I believe that happiness is an inside job, and that we are all responsible for our own, it does make sense that, with the passage of time, things change.

For lots of men older than 50, reaching material goals (having the confidence of security and a few toys) equals happiness, whereas many women of the same age will say that they were at their happiest being maternal, confident that they were fulfilling their purpose as a mother. Some women would argue that the reason they are less happy as they mature is because of the men they are with. One man interviewed on ABC News inappropriately suggested that it might be hormones. Although it is true that our brains produce the chemicals that create happiness (and if those systems are out of whack, a joyful existence can be elusive), neither gender has to be a victim of age or biology.

Not everyone reaches the same level of happiness; some people are just naturally more inclined to be happy. Just as with mental abilities or physical attributes, some of us have it, and some of us don't. But you do have some additional power to exert in the happiness area, if you choose to use it.

If you are not happy, find out what it is that makes you feel joyful and go after it. Don't divorce, have an affair, or quit your job today, but give the matter some serious thought, and first try to work with what you have.

List the pros and cons: Think about what life would really be like alone or what other kind of job you could do (or merely get). If you find family more fulfilling than work, create ways to be closer to those you love. If you believe that "he who dies with the most toys wins," then go get yours. Just remember that you can't do it at someone else's expense.

Tal Ben-Shahar, PhD, former professor of Harvard's most popular class ("Positive Psychology") and author of *Happier*, believes that being grateful for what we have, helping others, and building meaningful relationships are the keys to happiness. He also tells us that happiness comes from moving toward our goals and by filling our days with meaning and pleasure.

I truly believe that happiness is available to us all, no matter what our age, gender, or circumstances, but, as with most things of value in life, you have to work at it.

100. 10 Quick Reminders to Boost Your Self-Confidence

Confidence is my favorite antidepressant.
—Barton Goldsmith, PhD

Confidence is within us all, but sometimes, when the world is throwing you constant curveballs, it can get lost. Try using these tools the next time you are feeling less confident than you might like.

1. **Realize that self-confidence is not difficult to acquire.** But if you don't have enough, it can make succeeding in life hard. All you need are desire and persistence. A person grows whenever he or she thinks, contemplates, and dreams. Your ideas, reflections, and even random thoughts can build your self-confidence, but you have to be aware of them to get the full benefit.

2. **Do something for someone else.** Helping others lets you know that you are a good person and that you can use what you know in a positive way. The feeling that you get from giving to those less fortunate is priceless.

3. **Find the confidence that lies somewhere within.** Knowing that you are a person of honor and integrity keeps you on a purposeful and positive path. Those who have a strong moral fiber are generally confident people.

4. **Act "as if."** Acting as though life is already going your way can be a great psychological tool for building confidence. It allows you to physically and emotionally feel success in your body. You also send out a vibe that others pick up.

5. **Find a mentor.** If you didn't have the kind of parenting that helped you develop self-confidence, it's not too late. Find someone you respect, in a field you can love, and ask that person to be your mentor. Most people are flattered by the request and will do what they can to help you.

6. **Take good care of yourself.** Stay healthy, exercise, keep your energy high, and reward yourself appropriately for your achievements. If you are healthy, you can accomplish anything. If you are not, mere survival can be a challenge. Being

fit is very important to your confidence and your physical well-being. Exercise is your easiest, most accessible, and cheapest form of antidepressant. So don't just sit there and read about how good it is for your psyche as well as your body. Get up and get moving.

7. **Experience.** Having been there (and gotten the T-shirt) lets you know that you can go there again and again. Even if it has been years, most things in life are like riding a bike: You may be a little unsteady when you first try again, but the ability returns quickly. Remember that knowledge is power. If you get educated, and really learn what you are taught, no human being can throw you off track, because your connection to what you know is solid.

8. **Keep a confidence journal.** The process is elegant in its simplicity: Just write down five things you feel confident about. If you do it on a daily basis, journaling changes the way you think and feel. The best time is just before bed because the gratitude will flow into your subconscious as you sleep. Not only will you awake a bit more confident, but you will also be a tad happier.

9. **Build a support structure.** Support groups have been around much longer than psychotherapy. Medicine men would gather together and share their latest

tools, the women of ancient tribes looked after one another and the children, and individuals were allowed to seek council from the chief when required. If you don't have friends, family, or coworkers who support you emotionally, join a group or form one of your own.

10. **Monitor your thinking.** Of the gazillion thoughts we have a day, research has determined that 80 percent are negative. Science also tells us that we remember the negative because doing so was hard-wired into our DNA: We had to remember where the tar pits were so we wouldn't fall into them. Times are different now, and our thinking process has to evolve as well. Think positive thoughts.

Getting started may be the hardest part, so I suggest that now is the time to use these tips to turn things around. Make the effort, and you will feel the change sooner than you think. These tools work, but don't try to do all of them at once. Spend a few days working on one that resonates with you, and then try another. By doing so, you will feel more confident and much better about your life very soon. Learn how to rebuild and maintain your self-esteem; it is essential to having a fulfilled life. Things that make us question whether we are good enough will always come along; when it happens to you, these tools will get you back in touch with your personal power.

Index

About the Author

Honored by several professional associations, Dr. Barton Goldsmith is a three-time award-winning psychotherapist, a syndicated columnist and radio host, and a recognized keynote speaker. He has appeared on *CNN*, *Good Morning America*, *Fox & Friends*, *CBS News*, *NBC News*, *Beauty and the Geek*, and *The Greg Behrendt Show*.

Dr. Goldsmith was named by *Cosmopolitan Magazine* and in the book *The Complete Marriage Counselor* (Adams, 2010) as one of America's top therapists. In addition, his books, *Emotional Fitness for Couples: 10 Minutes a Day to a Better Relationship* (New Harbinger), which was published on Valentine's Day 2006, and the sequel, *Emotional Fitness for Intimacy: Sweeten and Deepen Your Love in Just 10 Minutes a Day*, released in April 2009, were included in the 2009 Academy Award and Emmy "Swag Bags." His most recent book, *Emotional Fitness at Work: 6 Strategic Steps to Success Using the Power of Emotion*, the third in the Emotional Fitness book series, was released by Career Press in September 2009 (and was also included in the Emmy gift bag). He was then asked to write this, his latest book.

He connects with audiences worldwide with his energetic, uplifting, and fun communication style. Not a button-down shrink, Dr. G (as he is referred to by his clientele) has a unique ability to inspire and entertain that leaves his readers, listeners, and those who attend his presentations always wanting more.

Since 2002, his weekly column, *Emotional Fitness*, which is syndicated by Scripps-Howard News Service, has been featured in more than 200 newspapers, including *The Chicago Sun-Times*, *The Orange County Register*, *The Detroit News*, and *The Atlanta Journal-Constitution*, giving him a substantial readership. Dr. G also hosts a weekly radio show on KCLU/NPR that airs in Los Angeles, Ventura, and Santa Barbara, California. He has been interviewed on numerous TV and radio shows, and for many publications; his expert advice is regularly featured in *Cosmo*. Recently, he served as the national spokesperson for the Mars Candy *My M&M's Treasured Moments Challenge*, and is currently writing a weekly blog for *Psychology Today*.

He received recognition from the City of Los Angeles for his work with survivors of the 1994 earthquake. *Emotional Fitness* was the winner of the Clark Vincent Award for Writing from the California Association of Marriage and Family Therapists. In addition, Dr. G received the Peter Markin Merit Award from the American Association of Marriage and Family Therapists for his humanitarian efforts. He has also been named the recipient of the Joseph A. Giannantonio II Award in recognition of his contributions as an Outstanding Educator in the field of addiction medicine, given by the California Association of Alcoholism and Drug Counselors. Dr. Goldsmith was a National Merit Scholar and a professor of psychology at Ryokan College, Los Angeles.

Dr. G began working in the field of psychology when his career in professional basketball was cut short because he only grew to 5-feet 6-inches tall.